HAROLD PINTER:
A Study of His Reputation (1958-1969) and a Checklist

by

Herman T. Schroll

The Scarecrow Press, Inc.
Metuchen, N.J.   1971

73-13304

Contents

Part I

Harold Pinter: A Study of His Reputation

I

In the eleven years between 1958 and 1969, the plays of Harold Pinter were produced an astounding number of times in England and the United States. Pinter's name has become well-known on stage, radio, television, and motion pictures. Critical writing about Pinter has, of course, kept pace with this rise in popularity. Regardless of a final judgment on his literary stature, he is currently, if only from this vast exposure and voluminous attention, a major figure in British theatre. The study of material about this playwright, however, not only teaches us a great deal about his plays, it also teaches us a great deal about the dramatic environment of the late 1950's and the 1960's. It is my hope that this study, by attempting to provide an overview of a broad spectrum of the critical writing about Pinter, will help to place both the criticism and the playwright in new perspectives.

The overall pattern of reactions to Pinter's plays is complex. The critical appraisal of the productions of the plays shifted from almost total rejection of the 1958 appearance of The Birthday Party to loud praise of the late 1960's productions; yet, even regarding the most recent productions, there remained a surprising element of critical ambivalence. Scholarly writing progressed from the relatively slight

5

quantity of the early sixties, which concentrated on Pinter's
use of a "room-womb" dramatic situation to create an atmosphere of terror, to the somewhat more numerous essays
of the mid-sixties which focused on the writer's use of
character relationships to create a poetic or symbolic social
criticism, and finally to the vast quantity of writing in the
late sixties which combed the entire Pinter canon for continuities or developments in techniques and philosophy.
Despite this rapid increase in the playwright's stature, the
scholarship also had been punctuated continually by denials
of his significance as a contemporary dramatist.

    Closer examination of this pattern reveals other
developments.   Reactions to the play productions showed a
growing fashionableness about Pinter.   Irving Wardle's ideas
about theatrical fashion, expressed in his article, "New
Waves on the British Stage, " may be helpful here; at the
very least, his ideas provide a haunting background for a
survey of Pinter criticism.[1] Theatrical fashion, Wardle
wrote, has a threefold pattern:

> a new play of unmistakable power appears on the
> scene;   it is taken up and given a position of dig-
> nity in a movement; the movement turns into an
> overblown cliché and is discarded together with
> the play.

Although Pinter had fallen into the grips of fashion, Wardle,
from his viewpoint of seven years ago, felt that Pinter's
basic value as a part of vital theatrical development had not
suffered.   However, similarities between the symptoms
Wardle listed and the characteristics of eleven years of
Pinter criticism point out that the playwright has continued
to be trapped by fashion.

    Wardle made one other observation that is relevant

to this discussion when he commented on the effects of
fashion. Fashion, he wrote, "has the effect of cancelling
out individual judgment in a way that makes you doubt the
validity of your reactions to any work, fashionable or not. "
After the transformation of a play, "its public reputation
intercedes between the spectator and the play--whatever his
opinion, there is danger that he will be reacting more to the
reputation than responding to the work. " The great acclaim
for Pinter, I find, exerted subtle pressures on critics; their
commentaries tended to follow common formulas, either
praising indiscriminately or inevitably raising particular objections. Such suspiciously repetitious reactions can only
strengthen Wardle's observation. Whether Pinter will survive
the fashion, however, still remains uncertain.

Yet other developments become apparent when criticism of Pinter is studied in detail. In her bibliography of
works about Pinter, Lois Gordon noted: "Pigeonholing the
works of Harold Pinter . . . seems to be a current pastime
for devotees of modern theater. " Commentators, indulging
in games of abstraction, loosely affixed such labels as
Comedy of Menace, Theatre of Cruelty, Theatre of Situation,
and Theatre of the Absurd, and such adjectives as naturalistic,
realistic, existential, supra-realistic, impressionistic, and
compressionistic. When frustrated by their inability to find
a label that would always fit, they considered Pinter sui
generis and coined the abstract terms "Pinterism" and
"Pinteresque" to describe him. Although treating the playwright as an individual might be seen as a positive step, too
often even these terms became limiting. They, too, were
expected always to fit, and when Pinter deviated from the
"Pinteresque" pattern, he was frequently criticized for failing to live up to the expected.

        Another pronounced trend in recent years was toward
oversubtle readings of Pinter's plays. Scholars projected
every word onto a symbolic screen. They quite literally
demanded that there be a "meaning," tangible and explicit,
significant and morally enlightening, in all of the plays; and
where they saw no deep meaning, they laboriously hunted one
out. Likewise, many scholars went beyond the meanings of
the individual plays to search for clearly-stated, well-formu-
lated Pinter philosophies of art and life. Engaging in these
studies, they repeatedly ignored or dismissed the playwright's
own explanation that he merely puts on paper what his characters say and do, that he writes with no conscious message
or symbolism. [2] Perhaps a greater irony was that, for all
of their work, few scholars of late offered new insights into
Pinter's plays; the bulk of the writing over these recent
years was merely a rewording of what had been said.

        In sum, then, this study will go beyond merely sum-
marizing criticism of Pinter to show some of the limiting
tendencies of the modern theatrical environment. In a large
sense, the critical reaction to Pinter is emblematic. Dramatic commentary, begun as an aid to an understanding of
the plays, finally lost its effectiveness as resulting theatrical
fashions prevented direct reaction to the plays and scholarly
interpretations became so abstract that their categories
hindered new ideas. Finally, the study will show a playwright's works being quite literally exhausted by over-
abundant critical enthusiasm compressed into too brief a
time span.

        Having outlined the purpose of this essay, I need to
explain its scope and organization. Only articles published
through autumn of 1969 about Pinter's plays and their productions will be discussed, and the latter will be limited

primarily to London and New York theatre productions and
to productions done on national radio and television.   The
reactions to all of his works, except Night School, Night
Out, and the revue sketches, will be surveyed.   These are
omitted for several reasons: they are definitely considered
minor works; they are seldom discussed in scholarly criticism; and except for the revue sketches, they have been performed only on British television and radio, and hence,
critical response is limited.

    The essay will be organized chronologically; it will
deal with the clusters of critical response to play productions within a year, or period of years, and then deal with
that year's, or period's, scholarly work.   Since I am chiefly concerned with larger trends, however, I will not follow
strictly chronological sequence within each smaller unit, but
rather will group the commentaries in a manner which will
most clearly show these trends.   Such organization approxi-
mates the manner in which the responses to Pinter unfolded.
Hence, I may take into account the massive influence that the
playwright's television and radio plays had on his popularity
and, in turn, on later reviewers.   Likewise, this method
allows me, without needless repetition, to show the stages
in critical reactions between 1958 and 1969 and to show when
particular ideas first appeared.

    I will concentrate on significant insights into Pinter's
techniques and themes, negative criticism of his works, and
clearly defined attitudes exhibited in the entire body of criticism.   Since many of the attitudes will necessarily be implicit, I will restrict my observations to those that are particularly persistent and relevant.   Although I may, at times,
quote comments that seem secondary to the major points of
reviews and articles, I point them out because they bring

out trends that are significant from a larger perspective.
If negative critical comments seem to predominate in later
discussions of reviews, such imbalance reflects chiefly a
decline in the number of original and significant insights into
new Pinter plays.

II

     The Birthday Party was first performed at the Arts
Theatre, Cambridge, and then moved to the Lyric Theatre,
Hammersmith, on May 19, 1958.   Critical scorn drove it
from the stage within the week.   The reviewer for the
London Times led a number of critics, calling the play "sur-
realistic drama" derivative of Ionesco.   The critic's major
objections were the play's obscurity and its characters'
lunacy.   Pinter, the critic wrote, looks for "theatrical effects out of . . . symbolic dialogue" but does not find it,
and hence, the play is neither funny nor terrifying, just puzzling and frustrating.
     Other reviewers, echoing these complaints, seemed to
challenge each other in reviling the play and the author.
J. D. Boothroyd of Punch called the play "a masterpiece of
meaningless significance"; and W. A. Darlington wrote in the
Daily Telegraph that the play, which "wallows in symbols and
revels in obscurity," was torture to sit through.   Spectator's
Alan Brien, likewise, saw the play as a poor Hitchcock
thriller within which Pinter "[has] failed to communicate";
and Cecil Wilson of the Daily Mail insinuated that Pinter
wrote the play to kill hours he spent in the dressing room
as an understudy.
     Several reviewers, trying to fight off utter confusion,

offered guesses at Pinter's theme. Myke Myson of the
Daily Worker saw the play as a power struggle between the
weak and the strong, but concurred that it was "another
evening of symbolism in the lunatic horror style." In his
Evening Standard review, Milton Shulman, on the other hand,
advanced a theory--"man's inability to stand up to the pow-
ers of verbal suggestion"--that pointed toward an allegory
about messengers of death; but he then dismissed this theory
as "naive." Likewise, Kenneth Tynan wrote in the Observer
that "the theme is that of the individualist who is forced out
of his shell to come to terms with the world at large." But
this idea, he also concluded, unfortunately was not new and
could easily have been said in fewer words.

Even at this early date, however, there were critics
who praised The Birthday Party almost unreservedly. In his
May 25 review, Harold Hobson, the Sunday Times' critic,
citing the absorbing theatricality of the play, its "fascinating"
characters, its "first rate" plot, its atmosphere of "delicious"
terror, staked his reputation on the assertion that Pinter
"possesses the most original, disturbing, and arresting talent
in theatrical London." Hobson saw the theme of the play as
"a primary fact of existence": "We live on the verge of
disaster . . . . It breathes in the air . . . . There is
something in your past--it does not matter what--which will
catch up with you." The fact that it is unknown adds to the
terror. Hobson closed by insisting that both the playwright
and the play "will be heard of again." In the Sunday Citizen,
Frank Jackson, likewise, called The Birthday Party "cheer-
ing." He found that the order of events in the play "could
not be more logical." Had Pinter been a foreigner, Jackson
concluded, his play would have been acclaimed: "But you
can't be British . . . and get away with mocking the formulas

so dear to us." Irving Wardle, some months later in
Encore, also praised Pinter's work for its theatricality. The
theatrical idea, Wardle asserted, comes to Pinter first:
"Mr. Pinter's way is the opposite of setting out deliberately
to embody a theme in action." But Wardle, nonetheless,
saw a theme in the play. Comparing The Birthday Party to
The Iceman Cometh, he wrote: ". . . the play demonstrates
that a man who has withdrawn to protect his illusions is not
going to be helped by being propelled into the outer world."

In a September 1958 Encore article, Wardle offered
more detailed criticism of The Birthday Party. He also
coined a term that dominated Pinter criticism in these
initial years. Wardle placed Pinter, along with other playwrights, as part of a "theatrical climate" characterized by
"dehumanized comedy." He labelled The Birthday Party a
"Comedy of Menace." In this play menace stands for
"destiny," an "incurable disease" which cannot be forgotten
and the end result of which is "violence approaching anarchy."
Wardle also pointed to the image that dominates the play:
"the womb."

Critical reactions to the two productions of Pinter's
works in 1959 were almost identical to the 1958 reactions.
On July 29, A Slight Ache was performed on radio on the
BBC Third Programme. Again reviewers felt the need to
find a deeper level to the play, and again the common charge
was that the play was completely meaningless. The Observer's reviewer, Paul Ferris, for example, admitted that
he did not understand more than the "cleverness" of the play
and proposed: ". . . say it's another of those plays where
the writer is telling us that identity and personality aren't
as stable as we think, but this isn't really much to discover
after an hour of intricate dialogue."

Positive remarks, though few, indicated a slightly greater tolerance for the playwright's style. The Times' critic, for one, noted the importance of the "ominous atmosphere" created by "manhandling commonplace utterance into fantasy." The critic also pointed to thematic similarities between A Slight Ache and The Birthday Party: both showed "the upheaval that occurs when an agent of the outer world enters a protected place." He commented, however, that the former play was not so "solidly built."

Writing about a Birthday Party production done in Ealing in December of 1959, A. Alvarez of the New Statesman also seemed slightly more familiar with Pinter's style. Alvarez called the play a "powerful, frightening, extremely funny" work that shows a "classic paranoiac set-up." Though this critic noted that symbols seemed unexplained, he offered a more detailed interpretation than any offered before: Goldberg and McCann stood for "respectable, smug and sinister agents of the Bitch Goddess, Success" who came to get Stanley, "the no-good artist and hopeless individualist." Stanley is destroyed finally in another kind of death, Alvarez wrote: ". . . he simply loses his power of self-expression: he can't speak."

Even in those first years of Pinter's exposure to the theatre public, several things that characterized the theatrical climate of the late 1950's were clear. All of the reviewers looked for deeper meaning in the play; they demanded that a clear-cut, coherent, symbolic statement be made in a play. The majority of the reviewers, who found no deep symbolism clearly evident, became outraged at Pinter. Yet other early critics, perceiving a theme, immediately lauded his plays as major expressions of truth about modern man, and they hailed him as a sign of life in the British drama.

Interestingly enough, in almost all cases, the reviewers concentrated on the same facets of the plays--character-
ization, dialogue, similarities to European writers, and obscure plotting--and simply approached these facets from opposite viewpoints: damning or praising. Such division of
opinion pointed to one of the fundamental controversies
dominating Pinter criticism throughout the eleven years of
this study: that of Pinter's significance. The reactions of
the majority of reviewers showed that while older criteria
for judging plays were gradually breaking down, the painful
change to new criteria was far from complete. The other
reactions already evidenced a predisposition for the creation
of a theatrical fashion in answer to the confusion brought
about by this change. Reviews from 1959 revealed an increased awareness of Pinter's creation of an atmosphere of
horror and comedy--observations that paralleled Wardle's
term, "Comedy of Menace," and that indicated the germina-
tion of the first movement with which the playwright was associated. Armed with this term, and the image of the room-
womb, critics soon began to cultivate a fashion, and they unfortunately continued to employ both the term and the image
long after Pinter moved on to other concerns.

III

1960 was the first year in which Pinter's plays received wide exposure in several media. Two of his early
one-act plays, The Room and The Dumb Waiter, were produced together at the Hampstead Theatre Club on January 21.
Although reception of the plays prompted a move to the more
public Royal Court Theatre on March 8, the overall tone of

reviews continued to be ambivalent. More critics liked the
plays than disliked them, but even those who praised had
reservations. The Times' reviewer of January 22, for
example, called the pieces "strange and subtle, " noting
Pinter's "taste for short, compressed forms" and comparing his plays to musical works. Although the critic considered The Dumb Waiter one of the "funniest and most disturbing" plays in London, he said that the precision of The
Room failed, leaving the final third of the play "utterly incomprehensible." Alan Pryce-Jones, writing in the Observer,
also praised the sobering emotional effect of the plays. He,
however, more closely pinpointed what he thought were the
failures of both plays: ". . . both are studies in treachery
and both are almost too conveniently polished off with a sudden act of violence." In The New Statesman, A. Alvarez
again focused on Pinter's ability to create terror and violence
in a dream-like world and to dramatize the "impossibility of
communication." However, feeling that the playwright concentrated too much on one "unchanging state of mind, a kind
of artistic hypnosis, " Alvarez already hoped for changes in
Pinter's next plays toward more general themes.

      Alan Brien perhaps summed up in his Spectator re-
view the ambivalent attitudes of most critics. He was even
more dogmatic about the faults of the plays, criticizing them
for trying to straddle two trends--realistic chunks of life
and "didactic impressionist chunks of comment"--and not
handling them together. The author still remained too "ob-
stinately a-plicit, " Brien wrote, and the task of the new
drama was "to be as specific and precise and explicit as
possible." Although Pinter's comment on "the horror of
the human condition" may be comically effective, "Mr.
Pinter must now start to answer his own questions."

Only one reviewer, again Harold Hobson, seemed to
embrace these pieces without reservation. In his January
31 review, he discussed the playwright's ability to captivate
audiences.   Pinter, Hobson wrote, provides "a view of life,
an individual world . . . in which it is not advisable to know
too much, in which the answers never fully meet the questions, and the effects are disconnected . . . slightly, but
. . . disturbingly from the causes." Such an "uncomfortable
world" paradoxically was, for Hobson, a "pleasure."

Several critics again noted Pinter's debts to the continental avant garde, implying that to realize this fact would
help one to understand his work. Patrick Gibbs of the Daily
Telegraph, for example, considered the plays similar in
theme to Waiting for Godot: they showed a preoccupation
with death and the purposelessness of life. Other reviewers
were primarily negative. The News Chronicle critic, Alan
Dent, and the Daily Worker critic confessed themselves baf-
fled, unable to guess what the author was trying to say, if
he was trying to say anything. David Nathan of the Daily
Herald, likewise confused, went further and denied Pinter
the label of "misunderstood genius."

Ambivalence was also apparent in reviewers' attitudes
toward The Birthday Party when it was done on television on
March 22, 1960. The response overall was markedly more
favorable than that to the first production, but critics still
questioned whether the play's success in creating an atmosphere was sufficient, and they looked for deeper significance.
The Daily Mirror's Richard Sear, for example, though he
called the play "astonishingly effective" in creating an atmosphere of horror through dramatization of "the childish
fears of unbalanced minds," admitted that he disliked its
attitudes. Other critics had even stronger reservations

about Pinter's ideas. Stewart Lane, though he found the
play "an eerily fascinating affair," wrote in the <u>Daily Worker</u>
that Pinter says nothing: ". . . you are left only with a
vivid impression of viciousness and cruelty in the abstract."
The acting and directing could only attempt to give the play
a "semblance of substance." Noticeable in Lane's last comment is an idea that became more pronounced in later years:
somehow, a number of reviewers felt, the acting of a Pinter
play determined how profound the play appeared; good acting,
they said, hinted at shadowy depths that Pinter may, or may
not, have actually intended. In the <u>Sunday Times,</u> Maurice
Wiggin, likewise, called <u>The Birthday Party</u> "an exercise of
talent in the void; invocation, rather than evocation, of
nameless dreads."

Still other reviewers were less receptive, sounding
reminiscent of the 1958 reviewers. Philip Purser, the
<u>News Chronicle</u> critic, for one example, criticized Pinter
for trying to "escape from social realism" by mixing human
elements in a random order. The play failed ultimately,
Purser said, because the audience didn't like or care about
Stanley. Other critics reiterated earlier complaints, calling
the play plotless, pointless, pretentious, and boring.

<u>The Birthday Party</u> provides an interesting case study
for what has been gradually happening in Pinter criticism.
Although there were still totally negative reviews, their
relative number had decreased over the year and a half.
Critics still sought symbolic themes, and most of their ambivalence stemmed from this search. But many more of them
were willing to listen long enough to allow the playwright's
atmosphere to grip them. Overall, this shift towards more
favorable criticism of <u>The Birthday Party</u> again revealed the
critics' tendency to create a fashion.

Pinter's second full-length play, The Caretaker, opening on April 27, 1960, at the Arts Theatre and subsequently moving May 30 to the Duchess Theatre, elevated the playwright to a more prominent position and probably marked the opening phase of the Pinter fashion. Praise of the play was much more unreserved; though some reviewers remained confused, they still recommended the play as a theatrical experience. Only one critic felt the play totally obscure. Those who praised it commonly singled out such aspects as the dialogue, the characterization, the mood, the theatricality, the production, and the acting of Donald Pleasance in the role of Davies. Frequently the play was compared to Waiting for Godot, a comparison that C.B. Mortlock wrote, The Caretaker could withstand in "full stature." For most critics, Pinter had shown, as T.C. Worsley wrote, that it was only "a step from extraordinary promise to extraordinary achievement."

Speculation about the play's theme was extensive. Many critics interpreted it on a symbolic, universal level. In his Observer review, Alan Pryce-Jones, for one, saw a tragic, lonely world in which the major problem was "individuality. How can we know who we are?" The Daily Telegraph's reviewer, Patrick Gibbs, also saw a "criticism of life" that was "rich . . . in pessimism"; possible themes he suggested were man's unpredictability, his inhumanity, and the unsatisfactory nature of human relations. Alan Dent of the News Chronicle found deeper symbolism: "Can it be that the old man is dead already when the curtain rises, and is just now about to realise the fact when the final curtain falls?" Irving Wardle in an Encore article wrote that The Caretaker was "obsessively concerned with human destructiveness," and he praised its "universality."

Other critics, not perceiving symbolic levels, offered
readings that concentrated on the author's picture of human
relationships.   In the Sunday Times, J.W. Lambert saw the
play expressing "an unuttered relationship of wary tenderness
between two brothers, and the bitterness of obligation, especially for those who have fallen lowest."   Kenneth Tynan, likewise, commented that The Caretaker is a "play about people," showing the "dry rot" of decrepit lower-class London-
ers.   Pinter, Tynan said, had finally moved his symbols and
paranoia into the background; and Tynan preferred not to hunt
for them.   Alan Brien, too, did not see "a symbol in the
house."   Rather there are here, he wrote, "three people em-
balmed alive in language."   The play shows that "the failure
of communication is often deadening, . . . but the success of
communication is nearly always fatal."

Negative comments were strong and, for the most
part, directed at aspects of The Caretaker that other critics
praised.   A great number of reviewers, disagreeing with
those who found significant themes, discovered faults in
Pinter's ideas.   Writing in Encounter, Nigel Dennis, for
example, called the play an "inadequate imitation" of Beckett.
The playwright, Dennis said, has no "vision" behind his
work; his world is "a fixed, grimy box" filled with "substantial idiocies."   The Daily Mail critic, Robert Muller,
likewise, wrote that although Pinter creates a compelling
world, ". . . it is, as yet, a world on a very small scale.
We must allow Pinter and his world to grow."   Marya
Mannes of the Reporter echoed this reservation when she
wrote that she failed to find "universality" beyond the play's
immediate situation.   Writing for the Hudson Review, Denis
Donoghue epitomized this objection to the play.   He branded
the play "untrue," "arbitrary, [and] unintelligent."   It "lies

when it says that people . . . are morons, thugs, imbeciles,
grunting their way through meaningless events." The Caretaker, he felt, as a "tragicomic parable of identity . . . is
falsely this, because the parable is rigged."

There were other revealing objections to the play.
Alan Brien noted that the play has "all [of Pinter's] now-
familiar ingredients" of menace, dreadful revelation, tension,
and grisly comedy. Other critics echoed Brien's comment.
In his New Statesman review, A. Alvarez again cited
Pinter's trouble as repetition from play to play: he now
seemed "more mannered than funny" and his terrors were
"too easily implied." J.C. Trewin of the Illustrated London
News, maintaining an earlier view that though Pinter wrote
good revue sketches he could not handle prolonged drama,
also claimed that Pinter was becoming predictable and "beginning to repeat himself" in dialogue, characters, and
techniques of mystification. For some reviewers, the
fashion grew old and boring the moment it began.

The Daily Worker and Punch critics raised an earlier
objection to Pinter's plays, asserting that they depended on
the acting for the impression of deep significance. Brilliant
acting, wrote the former, made the play "sound more impressive than I am sure it really was." Eric Keown, in
Punch, stated: "Badly acted [it] would be a nightmare; acted
as . . . it is [now] . . . it is an experience I shall not
quickly forget."

Reactions to the last Pinter work produced in 1960--
The Dwarfs, done December 2 on BBC radio--also reflected
the same approaches. Of the reviewers, only the Times'
critic liked the play. He saw a "striking extension of
[Pinter's] talent" as the author for the first time takes his
audience into the mind of one of his characters and uses the

"near insanity" of this character to add to the tension.   But
the play, said the critic, is unmistakably Pinter's: "what
we have come to expect of him" in terms of dialogue and
character.   The Observer's Paul Ferris was dissatisfied with
the same hero, who "carries the familiar mimeographed
label, D.C.T.W.A.H. (has difficulty in coming to terms with
world around him)."   The character comes "ready-made" to
the playwright; consequently, Ferris found him "tedious and
unimportant" because his situation "happens to be the
fashion."   Robert Robinson of the Sunday Times, sounding
like earlier reviewers, simply pronounced the play "boring"
because it lacked form.

        In addition to the direct questions raised by the
critics themselves, when all of the critical responses to The
Caretaker and the other plays produced this year are compared, the diversity of opinion on the same aspects of the
plays lead to further questions.   These issues quickly became, and continually remained, the center of the controversy
over Pinter.   Do his plays exist only on the level of surface
action, or do they have a symbolic level in the background?
Is his world only a specific, limited situation, or does it
have universality?   Is his comment on modern life true, or
is it forced and untrue?   Does Pinter have understanding and
compassion for his characters, or does he exhibit them as
cold, distorted specimens?   Are his plays furthering contemporary drama and capable of standing alone, or are they
poor imitations, lacking in uplifting moral vision?   Has
Pinter fallen into a predictable pattern of stage events, or
does he continue to challenge and surprise his audiences?
Do the plays owe their apparent depth to the author's
abilities, or does that depth come from superior actors?
While some of these issues may be trivial, others are basic

to any consideration of Pinter's final stature as a writer.

Commentators published a number of academic discussions on Pinter during 1960. For the most part, these
early articles merely elaborated on aspects of the plays that
had been discussed previously in reviews. Tom Milne in
an Encore article discussed The Birthday Party, with John
Arden's Sergeant Musgrave's Dance and John Whiting's
Saint's Day, as a "social" commentary concerned in particular with "the nature of violence." The violence in these
plays occurs between the alienated individual and the over-
powering society which crushes him. In the end, however,
". . . society, drained of its life-blood, slowly dies. . . ,"
itself an indirect victim of its own suppression.

John Arden, reviewing the published text of The Caretaker for the New Theatre Magazine, saw the play as a
"study of the unexpected strength of family ties against an
intruder." Echoing earlier comments, he wrote that there
was no need to hunt in a kind of intellectual "parlor game"
for deeper meanings. Though he considered the piece essentially realistic, Arden pointed out that this kind of realism
differed from that of Ibsen. Later in the year, Charles
Marowitz, in his "New Wave in a Dead Sea," also pointed to
a different type of realism in Pinter's plays. In contrast to
a social realism à la Wesker and Osborne, Pinter, like many
French dramatists, is concerned with "interior drives and
spiritual insights," a kind of interior realism. For these
latter writers, reality is "an endless swirl of living and
dying which ebbs and flows and never really stops." Consequently, Marowitz stated, these writers offer no conclusions to life. As Pinter explores a theme and its variations,
his "narrative exists for the sake of its ambiguity: sound
occurs for the sake of its echoes." Pinter says more in

this manner than most other writers say with direct statements, and, Marowitz concluded, he "remains the most
important playwright in the New Wave."

In a New Statesman article, H.A.L. Craig, on the
other hand, included Pinter in a discussion of "Poetry in
the Theatre." This new kind of prose poetry depends upon
the revelations and symbolism of moments on the stage:
"What you see or hear becomes an allusion to what is beyond being heard or said." Yet, Craig wrote, unlike
Beckett, who can create this poetry throughout an entire
play, Pinter is able to do so only "occasionally."

At this early stage, the academic writing followed
the critical reviews in concentration on the playwright's
message to the reader or audience, on the realism of his
characters and situations, and on the qualities of his dialogue. Here, too, despite more detailed analyses, there
was no agreement on Pinter's significance.

IV

Six productions of Pinter's works in 1961 showed
that, regardless of critical doubts, respect for the playwright continued to increase. In addition, Pinter was introduced to American audiences this year.

When A Slight Ache opened at the Arts Theatre,
London, as part of a triple bill (with plays by John
Mortimer and N.F. Simpson) on January 18, the response
again was two-fold: some reviewers revealed in their
praise the pressures of a theatrical fashionableness about
Pinter; others, in reaction to these pressures, raised a
number of earlier questions. The majority of the critics

praised the play, either without reservations or with only
minor reservations. Robert Muller of the Daily Mail, for
example, called A Slight Ache a "brilliantly sinister tour de
force," but neglected to explain why he felt it so. The
Daily Express' Bernard Levin wanted to know, "how with
such economy, does Mr. Pinter manage to create such pal-
patating terror in our hearts?" Harold Hobson became extremely lavish in his praise: "Any ten lines of these plays
contain more wit, more sense of reality, more human feeling, more richness of imagination, more toughness of in-
telligence, and more sheer entertainment than the whole of
all the new drawing-room comedies presented in London during the last two years."

        Other critics had reservations and remained luke-
warm. The Times' reviewer could not consider the play
"important" in the playwright's work. Because Pinter sends
the audience home "to decide . . . exactly what it has been
about," the play remains only "an essay in a form of sus-
pense that [Pinter] has made his own." Milton Shulman
called it "smaller and less satisfying" than other Pinter plays.
"Uncommitted to any political or social solution of the contemporary dilemma," it attempts only to create "atmosphere"
and finally is just another of "Pinter's familiar exercises
in abstract terror."

        The reviewers who objected to A Slight Ache again
generally cited the same examples listed by those who liked
the play. Several, like W.A. Darlington of the Daily Telegraph, castigated Pinter for being at "his most determinedly
obscure." Bamber Gascoigne wrote in his Spectator review
that Pinter's writing keeps hinting at a deeper meaning
which is not there. Perhaps, he speculated, the playwright
may be "pulling the wool, fouling up the scent." J.C.

Trewin offered undoubtedly the most scathing criticism of
A Slight Ache. He summed up clearly what other reviewers
had been saying obliquely, and pointed to an issue which continued to grow more prominent in later criticism. Trewin
dismissed the piece as "just silly," a creation of "weari-
ness." "[Pinter's] style by now is getting old-fashioned,"
he wrote. "You know--the comic macabre: suggest a lot,
mean little, and leave it to your audience." Two of the
earlier questions received additional emphasis in these reviews: Has Pinter fallen into a repetitious and boring pattern? Does he have a relevant, human viewpoint? These
two particular issues repeatedly became focal points of
argument combating the pressures of the growing fashion.

    The next two major productions of Pinter's plays
were on television: The Collection on May 11, 1961, and
The Dumb Waiter on August 10, 1961. The responses to
each production generally centered on the issues thus far
pointed out. Several critics considered The Collection
"light-weight Pinter." Noting disparities between this work
and others, many commentators discussed the author's shift
from working-class characters to middle-class characters.
The Times Literary Supplement's critic offered the only significant comment on this shift: ". . . one had always supposed that Mr. Pinter took as his subject modern man in
general rather than modern working-class man . . . . "
Another reviewer, the Daily Telegraph's Eric Shorter, however, saw The Collection simply as still "the Pinter world
of horrors."

    Several critics offered statements of the author's
theme, both for this play and for others in general. The
Times Literary Supplement's reviewer saw Pinter using ambiguity and contradiction to call into question the concept of

truth; the Sunday Times' critic, Maurice Wiggin, saw a
"parable" on the "biblical theme which suggests that whoever
lusts after a woman with his eyes has committed adultery";
and the Daily Mail's critic, Peter Black, saw the play as
"an almost painfully explicit study of jealousy."

Again reviewers argued over the usual facets of the
play. For some, the dialogue clearly advanced the central
concerns of the play; for others, it was a veil used to
create needless ambiguities. Several commentators saw the
play as evidence of life in the theatre and a continuation of
Pinter's dramatic development while others oriented their
comments around what they had come to expect from the
playwright. The latter critics found the same menace and
ambiguities, the same types of characters, the same world,
the same theme of intrusion, and the same techniques for
presenting clues. Phil Diack, the one totally negative reviewer, went even further, writing that the play "[shows]
Pinter's remarkable talent exhausted beyond the point of
self-parody."

Again for The Dumb Waiter there was much praise
intermingled with admitted confusion. Only Maurice Wiggin
of the Sunday Times offered an interpretation, citing the
theme of "boredom." The Times' critic, on the other hand,
criticized the particular production, concluding that it was
"a pity, for properly treated the play is one of Mr. Pinter's
best." Other reviewers dismissed the play as almost completely confusing, lacking clear ideas or themes; or they
limited themselves to comments on its dramatic effectiveness.
Wiggin indirectly offered a comment on the process of theatrical fashion. He wrote that once the viewer understood
Pinter's "Alice in Wonderland trick of turning logic inside
out, or rather of applying low-worldly realism to other-

worldly fantasy," the playwright's work became "amusing" and "watchable."

Although The Birthday Party had been done in San Francisco during the summer of 1961, the first major Pinter production in the United States opened on October 4, 1961, when The Caretaker was brought, virtually intact, from London to Broadway. The reactions of American critics closely paralleled those of the British critics a year before. The few differences in responses were in directions easily anticipated: far more ecstatic praise, greater aware- ness of Pinter's own comments on his art, more determined searching for significant meaning in the play, and consider- ably fewer, but more serious, reservations from reviewers who disliked the play.

Words of praise ranged from "strangely compelling beauty" to "thoroughly enthralling," from "tender" to "shattering." Almost unanimously, commentators, whether or not they liked the play, whether or not they thought it had deep significance, praised its theatricality. They also lauded the climax, the comedy, the characterization, the dialogue, and the ambiguity.

Although the New York reviewers gave more overt notice of their awareness of Pinter's own comments on his writing--that he does not write allegories or parables, that he writes only for the theatre--they most often mentioned the author's disclaimers prior to explaining the deeper symbolism they had found. Several critics, however, took The Caretaker at its theatrical level, either in deference to Pinter's or their own ideas. Henry Hewes in the Saturday Review, for example, felt no need to find hidden allegories since the play lives in "the absolute urgency of the stage action." Commonweal's Richard Gilman also saw The

Caretaker as a "straightforward drama." The three characters constitute "a triad roughly on the order of the
brothers Karamazov--the major faculties of man's being."
Yet, wrote Gilman, these men are not symbols, but rather
"mysterious new creations."

Other commentators refused to heed Pinter's statements. Howard Taubman of the New York Times, in his
October 15 review, wrote that although the characters are
personalities, not symbols, and although the playwright
claims we should not interpret, the play is so deep and so
full of genius that we must interpret. Whatever Pinter's
intentions, the play is so well-written that the "larger
meanings take care of themselves." In his two reviews
then, Taubman interpreted the themes of the play as "the
malaise of contemporary society" and the "Gethsemane" of a
piece of "human jetsam." Harold Clurman wrote in the
Nation that the play suggests "ideological patterns" which "call
for interpretation" despite the author's protests. Clurman
then advanced an allegorical reading in which Mick is "a
kind of godhead--angel and devil in one," Aston is "a sort
of Christ figure," and Davies, trying to "prove who he
'really' is," can "stand for mankind itself." The final verdict of The Caretaker, Clurman said, is that Davies must
be disposed of. Writing in the Educational Theatre Journal,
John Gassner also expressed dissatisfaction with Pinter's
denials of allegory: "The author's disclaimer of any sub-
surface reality in his play may have been motivated indeed,
precisely by an understandable reluctance to have to live up
to allegorical expectations." However, Gassner wrote, the
play does have a workable symbolism, hinted at rather than
logically defined. His symbolic interpretation followed the
same Devil-Christ-Man pattern that Clurman formulated.

The majority of the reviewers of The Caretaker paid
no attention to Pinter's disavowals, and they offered widely
varying statements of the play's theme; for the most part,
they reasserted the themes of communication, loneliness,
fear of the void, and failure of relationships with few new
insights.   The interpretation offered by the Time magazine
critic perhaps exemplified most of these readings.   This
reviewer saw "several levels of meaning" in the play.   Psy-
chologically, Pinter gives us a tragedy of "isolation": men,
"paralyzed by failures of will and nerve," who are victims
of their own delusionary hope of self-therapy and their own
"self-concern."   Philosophically, the play is "a telling re-
statement of man's eternal aloneness";   and politically, it
is a "parable of humanity's pressing international predicament."   Only a few commentators offered different interpretations.   Christian Century's Tom F. Driver, for one
example, saw the play as a presentation of the "almost un-
bearable anguish" of a character going mad. In the end, however, there is no laughter at this joke played by existence,
only fear and pain: "Nothingness cannot laugh.   For laughter
you have to have Being.   So The Caretaker does not begin in
nihilism . . . but that is where it ends."

Objections to The Caretaker mirrored British objections of the year before.   The primary difference was that
most negative criticisms came balanced with praise or were
only passing comments in essentially favorable reviews.
John McClain of the Journal American, for example,
stated that "most of the credit for the power of the play
must be accorded the cast for extremely persuasive per-
formances."   Richard Gilman criticized Pinter for not being
sufficiently "absurd" or "untraditional" in his treatment of
the brothers: "That is to say, his play is too much a thing

of jarring styles, characterizations and motivations, not a
consistent piece of relentlessly exhibited discovery . . . . "
Thomas R. Dash wrote in Women's Wear Daily that the play
"might have been compacted into a one-act psychological
study, but padded out with a great deal of repetitious stuff-
ing, it is not easy to take for three whole acts."

    Other critics again based their reservations on what
they took to be the play's content. John Gassner was sus-
picious of what he called Pinter's "negativism." Robert
Coleman found Davies only "a vicious, shiftless ingrate" and
the other characters "maladjusted." "We just don't believe
that drab, mixed-up people make for stimulating or reward-
ing theatre," he wrote in the Mirror. "We like our slices
of life cut from the top and not the lowest strata of humanity." Robert Brustein, writing in New Republic,
epitomized these objections to the author's vision of the
world. He saw Pinter selecting "naturalistic details" in a
manner that distorts them: ". . . the play is a slice of
life, sliced so arbitrarily that it has lost all resemblance
to life." Because the playwright excludes "thought and feeling" from the work and presents details that have no relation to "any known form of human life," he creates "a
naturalism of the grotesque."

    Of course, some commentators gave Pinter no credit.
The reviewer for Variety curtly dismissed the play as "an
example of garrulous unintelligibility"; and John Simon wrote
in Hudson Review that the playwright, who "has no style, no
ideas, no poetic fantasy with which to hold us," relies upon
his knowledge of "the externals of theatre and his shallow
awareness of contemporary trends in drama." Simon's
comment, in addition, revealed in a negative manner an
awareness of the pressures of the theatrical fashion.

Although the response of the New York critics closely paralleled the London critics', there were visible changes.
The decrease in the relative number of totally negative reviews served as an index of the playwright's increasing
stature.   The New York reaction to The Caretaker was
a logical outcome of earlier trends in criticism.   When
Pinter arrived on Broadway, he came with the loud fanfare
of being called by many of his countrymen England's fore-
most playwright.   In addition, the publication of his plays
by Methuen in London and Grove Press in New York during
1960 and 1961 added to this estimate.   Pinter had also been
the subject of several published interviews and several
television interviews prior to the opening of The Caretaker.[3]
The American reviewers consequently were more prepared
for Pinter and more readily willing to accept him as an
established and growing playwright.   Hence, they offered
more subtle readings, and almost every critic found something positive to say about the play.   Yet, the sum of the
entire year's criticism, particularly the vocal negative
comments that always appeared, showed surprisingly little
movement toward resolution of the central issues.

The scholarly work on Pinter in 1961 continued the
analyses begun in earlier commentaries.   The quality of
the playwright's realism remained a major issue.   In his
"Accepting the Illusion," John Bowen classed Pinter, on
the basis of his dialogue, as a realist: "his observation
may be appalled [sic], but it is exact."   But Bowen, like
earlier critics, felt such realism insufficient.   Pinter
needed to change; he could not "go on saying the same
thing over and over again."   The author of a Times Literary Supplement article, "The Reaction Against Realism,"
wrote that Pinter, unlike other current playwrights who

were revolting from realism, exhibited in his later plays a
"consistent move . . . closer and closer to reality." Yet,
although he had begun to deal with more "fairly normal"
human beings in "fairly recognizable surroundings," his
realism still had overtones from the "more perilous reaches
of the imagination."

In two 1961 publications, Martin Esslin explained
more fully Pinter's qualified realism. Esslin also created
a second label--"Theatre of the Absurd"--that provided im-
petus for the Pinter fashion. In an article in Twentieth
Century, Esslin explained the Theatre of the Absurd and
told how Pinter fitted into this dramatic trend. Through
poetic theatrical images, these playwrights expressed "the
loss of the feeling that the world makes sense, or can be
reduced into an integrated system of values." There
was, wrote Esslin, no contradiction between the absurd and
realism: "By transcribing reality with ruthless accuracy
the dramatist arrives at the disintegrating language of the
Absurd." Pinter is "preoccupied with man at the limits of
his being" where he faces the problems of self and of coming to terms with reality. When he concentrates on "the
individual's pathetic search for security, [on] secret dreads
and anxieties, [on] the terrorism of our world . . . ,
[on] the tragedy that arises from lack of understanding
between people on different levels of awareness," he seeks,
rather, a "higher degree of realism." Such concerns with
a poetic realism in the Theatre of the Absurd, Esslin
wrote, might make it "more enduring" than plays of social
realism, which presented a false and shallow picture, tied
to the fluctuations of social and political circumstances.

In his book, The Theatre of the Absurd, Esslin expanded the same lines of interpretation, treating individual

plays more extensively and including discussions of more
recent plays. Although he made no new points, Esslin added an important observation on Pinter's stature, an observation that may well have been overlooked in the Pinter
scholarship of the sixties: "The quantity of [Pinter's] output
and his rise to success are truly astonishing, but he is far
too young to allow anything like a summing up of his achievement or a final verdict on his place in British drama."
However, on the basis of this "early phase," Esslin felt it
possible "to say that he has already won himself an important place among the playwrights of this century."

Other articles dealt with particular themes in Pinter's
plays. Mark Cohen, in a book review of A Slight Ache and
Other Plays, discovered several previously unnoticed threads.
He noted as recurring themes in the plays: "the middle-
aged mixture of the maternal and the sexual" in female characters, "parallel forms of male dominance" in the male
characters, and "the solid manifestation of respectable reality" that is threatened in the room. On the other hand,
Kay Dick, in her "Mr. Pinter and the Fearful Matter,"
analyzed in greater detail what had been noticed in earlier
reviews: the fears of Pinter's characters. She found that
they are primarily "fearful of the social consequences of
intimacy and communication."

Academic writing, like the production reviews, addressed a general question: What is Pinter doing? As
with the reviewers' conclusions, the scholars' conclusions
depended upon the particular viewing angles. The major
difference apparent in the increasing volume of scholarly
writing was the implicit assumption that the playwright was
a worthy literary subject. The weight of such material
about Pinter tended over the years to create a self-

fulfilling prophecy: since so much had been written about
him, later commentators felt that he had to be great. Most
were falling into the fallacy that Esslin noted: they failed
to reserve judgment until time enough had passed. The irony
was that the popular and academic praise of Pinter grew
despite the continual reservations that were voiced. In other
words, basic questions about the playwright's talents, techniques, and significance were never resolved because his
stature as a fashionable playwright intervened.

   The academic discussions also pointed out clearly the
tendency toward pigeonholing. Esslin, with his term,
"Theatre of the Absurd, " began more than he was aware of
at the time; a term meant as a flexible guide soon became
a rigid category.[4] Interestingly, that category was soon op-
posed to realism as a category, despite Esslin's clear link-
ing of the Absurd with a realistic view of the world. The
label, "Theatre of the Absurd, " became one category in an
abstract debate over Pinter's works. "The Theatre of Social
Realism" became another; and even the earlier term that
Wardle coined, "Comedy of Menace, " continued to reappear.
Other critics, unable to resolve the conflicts between these
terms, quickly attempted to define middle categories and to
coin new terms to describe the playwright's work.

                                  V

   Although The Collection had been done on television
in May of 1961, it received its greatest critical attention in
1962 when it was done on radio June 12 and 30 and opened
at the Aldwych Theatre, London, on June 18. The criticism
of these productions brought few new developments. Most

often critics saw the theme of the play as the nature of
truth. As Milton Shulman of the Evening Standard expressed
it, the play is "a commentary on the inability of any of us
to recognise the truth." Other commentators saw Pinter
concerned with a wide range of themes: love, infidelity, the
power of personality, the impossibility of communication,
upper-middle class manners, and the conflict between personal and social identities. In reaction to the fashionable
praise, of course, several reviewers again expressed boredom and utter confusion.

A number of critics commented directly on the ad-
Negative criticisms again ranged widely. Often
critics found the piece disappointing because they saw it as
light or trivial, or because they thought the playwright made
too overt use of his usual "tricks." As Peter Wilsher
asked in his Sunday Times review: ". . . Mr. Pinter's trip
to Leeds surely represents a distant retreat from the great
roaring abyss of human inadequacy he has been mapping so
memorably up to now?" Other criticisms leveled at The
Collection were: dull situation, insignificant and shallow
characters, maddening pauses in the dialogue, and failure
to sustain mood.

A number of critics commented directly on the adverse effects of Pinter's growing familiarity. W.A. Darlington wrote that as the author's touch grew more sure and as
audiences learned his idiom, "the flavour of his subtle sense
of comedy grows less tantalizing." The Daily Express'
Herbert Kretzmer also noted that audiences were becoming
too "cosy" with the playwright's style: "Nothing will destroy
Mr. Pinter's effects and influence more swiftly than this
kind of public cosiness, since it completely destroys the
kind of hallucination that haunted his earlier plays . . . . "
As if further to establish the point of Pinter's fashionable-

ness, critics increasingly used such words as "Pinterland"
and "Pinterese." Even Darlington exhibited the effects of
the fashion when he referred to "highly Pinteresque conver-
sations."

Other commentators directed attention to the possibility
of self-imitation in Pinter's techniques. In the Observer
Irving Wardle noted that "evasion of communication" could
become "simply a technique for fabricating dialogue." He
wrote: "When this kind of trick is pulled too often one stops
bothering about formal balance and interplay of motifs and
starts to long for content." Bamber Gascoigne, likewise,
warned in his Spectator review that Pinter shows "signs
. . . of parodying himself, falling back on the clichés of the
theatre of the absurd."

The debates over labels continued. Like Gascoigne,
Stephen P. Ryan, the critic for America, identified Pinter
with "Theatre of the Absurd." Paul Mayersberg, in a more
lengthy article in the Listener, compared Pinter and Ionesco
in order to show that the former is "not a dramatist of the
Absurd." Reality in The Collection, Mayersberg wrote,
is "social reality," in which characters are "precisely motivated" by "social attractions."

The Collection also received its first American exposure when it opened off-Broadway in November of 1962 with
The Dumb Waiter. The New York critics' reactions differed
little from those of the London critics', and these responses
also revealed a growing familiarity with Pinter. As in the
case of The Caretaker, American reviewers gave a greater
number of lengthy statements of praise devoid of cogent remarks on the new piece. While a few commentators expressed puzzlement in the midst of praise, most guessed at
the playwright's themes. For the most part, their

speculations, though phrased differently, mirrored earlier
British ideas: self-deception, cruelty, interpersonal relationships, alienated man, and the uncertainty of truth. Two
reviewers, Walter Kerr and Harold Clurman, found different
themes, respectively, the "problem of transposed identities"
and "a protest, albeit a hopeless one, against the pressure
of our industrial civilization."

Negative criticism of the works also echoed the discontent usually associated with Pinter plays. To a large
extent critics compared the two one-act plays to the Caretaker production they had seen the year before, and they
concluded that the former were not so great an achievement.
To some, like Clurman, these plays seemed without emotional depth: "The Caretaker, for all its effort to suppress it,
has feeling; The Collection, almost none."

Other reviewers tried to express differently how they
felt the author had failed. The reviewer for Variety wrote
that the plays are "not Pinter at his best" because they are
"uneven, seemingly lacking in substance"; in a sense, The
Collection, for example, is "a triumph of technique over subject matter." Richard P. Cooke also pointed this out in the
Wall Street Journal: ". . . there are times when the author
seems to become the prisoner of his own technique."

Yet other critics commented on the imperfection of
Pinter's world view. Richard Gilman felt that although the
playwright pointed to the emptiness in our world, he needed
to fill in some of the vacancies: his images "are skeletal
and unfinished, as though they have known what not to be but
do not yet know what to become." Ned O'Gorman, writing
in Jubilee, angrily accused Pinter of writing about "a uni-
verse where joy is sadism, flagellation and the various
techniques men have learned of how to prey on one another."

Beneath the accomplished dialogue, O'Gorman stated, was
"the dry rot of a stricken language, banal violence and
existential prattle."

The sum of the entire year's reviews showed Pinter
becoming more trapped in the rigid mold of fashion. Although a substantial number of reviewers continued to find
nothing in Pinter's works but deliberate obfuscation, most
expressed their growing familiarity with the playwright in
certain ways: they assumed that they had found a pattern
to Pinter's art; when a new play seemed to conform to these
preconceptions, they chortled about the "Pinteresque" effects
that created "Pinter-land." Once reviewers established
clearly that the new play fitted into the mold, they ceased to
look at the play itself. Preoccupation with fashion, however,
had other adverse effects. Patterns became a rather limiting yard-stick for assessing the newly experienced play。
The Collection and The Dumb Waiter were, thus, often seen
as failing to measure up to, or to extend, the Pinter fashion
and were dismissed as "minor" plays. Further, belief in
a rigid Pinterism helped reviewers to accuse the author of
self-parody and of putting techniques before subject. Lastly, a pattern easily prompted symbolic or allegoric projection and led critics to complain of Pinter's world view.
Thus, they dictated that, in order to become a major
dramatist, he had to provide answers within the contexts of
a larger, more mature world.

The volume of academic writing on the playwright
ballooned rapidly in 1962. However, scholars, for the most
part, merely continued to categorize Pinter's work, hoping
to make it more understandable. As mentioned earlier, the
debate at this point, apart from minor labels, revolved
around three categories: Comedy of Menace, Realism (or

Naturalism), and Absurd; however, this year scholars created a hybrid category (often called Hyper-realism or Supra-
realism by later commentators) from the latter two. Those
scholars who did not become involved in this labeling game
most often theorized about other aspects of the playwright's
art that had been mentioned by other commentators.

Two scholars saw Pinter's plays as realistic. In a
Tulane Drama Review article, Ossia Trilling described the
author as a well-established member of a new English
realist movement that portrayed the "refusal of common man
to be put upon by the mumbo-jumbo . . . of the new society
. . . seeking anew to enslave his free spirit." John Russell Taylor, in his The Angry Theatre, offered a more detailed analysis. He likewise saw Pinter's plays, unlike
most post-Look Back in Anger plays, becoming "more and
more realistic." Taylor discussed three phases in the playwright's development: from "comedies of menace" that
dealt with confined surroundings threatened from the outside,
to middle plays that dealt with "failures of communication,"
and finally to a "psychological realism" in which "a simple
truth can often be something more terrifying than ambiguity
and doubt." Since Pinter's aim finally was to show that
"there are no clear-cut explanations for anything," Taylor
noted that the writer's work paradoxically "often seems
least realistic when it is closest to actuality." Yet, Taylor
seemed to qualify this position in an article for World
Theatre. Pinter created, he said, "paradoxically an
hallucinatory super-realism in the very process of apparently
abandoning realism altogether."

Arthur Ashworth, on the other hand, identified Pinter
with the Theatre of the Absurd, which, he wrote, involved
a "complete rejection of realism." Ashworth qualified this

statement somewhat, however, when he discussed Pinter specifically. This playwright, Ashworth wrote, belonged "more to the realist theatre" than other writers of the absurd. Into a nucleus of realistic characters in a "real life" situation, Pinter introduced "one or more characters that he builds in non-realist terms"; thus he twisted the realistic situation askew and created nightmare.

As Taylor's and Ashworth's qualifications indicated, scholars found it difficult to place the playwright cleanly in either the realistic or absurd theatres. Consequently, they more often saw Pinter starting with an essentially normal viewpoint and then creating a world that in some way transcended the normal. Jacqueline Hoefer, for example, explained that The Birthday Party depends upon "elements of conventional realism" which through Pinter's handling slowly "[acquire] symbolic meaning." Thus, she took the struggle between the outside forces (Goldberg and McCann) and the individual (Stanley) to be symbolic of a tradition-weighted society coming to reclaim the alienated artist who is accused of "social betrayal." In his "The Theatre of Harold Pinter," Bernard Dukore, likewise, wrote that the playwright's world was "realistic, after a fashion" as it pictured "contemporary man beaten down by the social forces around him." Though Pinter used elements from the real world, the overall pattern was unreal and grotesque. Dukore explained: "Pinter's plays have an unreal reality, or a realistic unreality." Kenneth Muir, with different emphasis, wrote in his article, "Verse and Prose," that Pinter created an "unrealistic drama" out of a prose poetry; using "dialogue superficially colloquial to express neurosis, madness and terror," Pinter provided a "total effect [that] is Kafkaesque and terrifying."

Essentially unconcerned with the controversy over categories, a number of scholars offered views of Pinter that elaborated on earlier comments of reviewers. Ruby Cohn, discussing "The World of Harold Pinter," wrote that he created "dramas of dehumanization" that implied the importance of humanity. His plays showed in the end the "virtual annihilation of an individual" caught in the "wriggle for existence." In an essay in Contemporary Theatre, Clifford Leech discussed Arnold Wesker and Harold Pinter in terms of a relationship similar to that between two other Romantics--Wordsworth and Coleridge. Wesker, like Wordsworth, cultivates an "atmosphere of actuality" as he tries to see common surroundings more sharply. Pinter, on the other hand, like Coleridge, concentrates on events and characters "altogether strange" yet with a "semblance of truth" as he shows a world that is "always old, shabby, sick."

Attempting to rethink the traditional categories of comedy, tragedy, and tragicomedy in his The Dark Comedy, J.L. Styan identified Pinter with Beckett and Ionesco as creators of a "comic danse macabre." In a sense, Styan elaborated on the idea of a Comedy of Menace that, "through an exquisite friction of nightmare and normality, [shows] the earthly human need for security, recognition and acceptance." Laurence Kitchin coined a new term in Mid-Century Drama to explain a different view of the same process. The playwright arrives at social comment through what Kitchin termed "Compressionism": the characters are placed in a room, or enclosed space, and then "their essence is squeezed out under pressure."

R.D. Smith's comments in his "Back to the Text" became especially relevant in the light of the volume of writing about Pinter that had accumulated through the end

of 1962. Too often, Smith wrote, modern writers are
"clumped together in schools and movements by critics who
so save themselves the bother of finding out what each individual writer is saying." This leads critics to an appreci-
ation of criticism rather than to "the exertion of actually
reading and experiencing a work." Terms such as Commitment, Non-Communication, Anti-Human Pessimism, Smith
felt, distort plays and hinder audiences. The problem, for
example, of a term such as "Non-Communication" when applied to Pinter's work is that his plays "communicate tri-
umphantly in a great many languages." In answer to those
who accused the playwright of creating a barren world, Smith
wrote that only a bad reading could "ignore the charge of
human feeling that animates these mis-called 'pessimistic'
plays." Smith's final challenge to all critics was to go
"back to the text."

Smith's commentary provided a meaningful gloss on a
year that brought increased negative criticism of a "Pinteresque" style and of "Pinterism" and that saw more determined attempts by scholars to pigeonhole the author within
a rigidly defined category. Such warnings against abstract
formulations, needless to say, also applied to critics whose
enthusiasm for Pinter contributed to the fashionable movement against which others reacted. Perhaps a great deal of
the confusion and the disagreement in assessments of the
playwright stemmed from the relative impossibility of treating any play as an abstraction without in some way distort-
ing it.

VI

The Lover was done on television on March 28, 1963,
and subsequently opened with The Dwarfs at the Arts The-
âtre, London, on September 18, 1963. Although most
critics praised the first production, calling it one of the best
television offerings in a long time, few of them made any
effort to look for symbolic meanings. The majority saw
the piece examining a marriage relationship and showing
interrelationships between fantasies and imagination. Only
the Times' reviewer found more than the surface concern
with marriage fantasies; he noted that Pinter continues his
preoccupation "with fragmentation of human personality."

Other reviewers made the usual comments. Richard
Sear could see "no message" in the play. Philip Purser
noted that the revelation is "predictable" and that by "Pinter
standards it [is] an easy, even lightweight piece." Stewart
Lane saw the play "laden with sexual symbolism" but "all
in all" as "little more than a Pinterish exercise."

When The Lover and The Dwarfs opened on stage,
however, reviewers speculating about the theme of The Lover
delved considerably further than the superficial examination
of marriage. T.C. Worsley, writing in the Financial
Times, saw the play revealing how much "perversion" there
is in "so much so-called normal sexuality." Similarly,
Ronald Bryden discussed The Lover in the New Statesman
as a criticism of "the contradictory liberal axioms of sex
by which we moderns try to operate." Pinter poses the
question: Can the "ideal marriage" include "the whole dark
continent" of the "sexual subconscious?" Encore's Stuart
Hall also saw a "hopelessly civilised" marriage. At the
end of the play, however, Hall found a "reconciliation" that

brings new rules and "'true' lives" to the game; hence, it
was for him "profoundly, deeply optimistic."

Some reviewers attempted to deal with both plays together. The Times' critic, for example, saw in the plays an
"incurable obsession with the elusiveness of reality." Likewise, Philip Hope-Wallace wrote in the Guardian that "both
plays are concerned with ontology: the department of meta-
physics which deals with 'the essence of being in the abstract.' In other words, . . . who are you, and are you
you when you are with other people or only a projection of
their idea of you?"

Negative criticism of The Lover and The Dwarfs here
most strongly reflected the unvarying assumptions about
Pinter's art. Most reviewers, professing utter confusion
about The Dwarfs, discounted it as an experiment that failed.
The most frequent complaint was that the play failed the-
atrically because of descriptive writing, abstractions, far-
fetched imagery, and a lack of dramatic urgency. Several
critics were less complimentary. Stuart Hall wrote that
The Dwarfs totally lacked "conviction" and became a "sort
of romantic mish-mash expressionism"; and Jack Lewis,
the Sunday Citizen's reviewer, branded the play "formless
rubbish" which "appears to have nothing to do with anything
at all."

Other negative criticism, directed at both plays,
seemed to be based upon a perception of stagnation in
Pinter's work. The Daily Worker's critic saw the playwright wasting his talents in a "dead end of fantasy and
despair." Milton Shulman in the Evening Standard accused
Pinter of "marking time in his own private, padded cul-de-
sac," writing plays "far inferior" to his earlier ones. The
Sunday Telegraph critic specifically complained that the

author "has learned so well how to show characters failing
to communicate truly with each other, that he is forgetting
to communicate with us."

The frequency with which "Pinter" words were used
generally increased with the reviewers' dissatisfaction. Such
words continued to indicate strong preconceptions of Pinter's
work. Although he liked both plays, Philip Hope-Wallace in
the Guardian referred to The Lover as a piece of "pure
Pinterism." With quite the opposite attitude, Herbert
Kretzmer of the Daily Express called the play "a neat, hor-
rific little Pintermime, full of those now familiar pauses
and slow sidelong glances proper to the form." W.A. Darlington confessed his frustration in a string of epithets:
"Pinter was pinting like mad"; The Lover was "fairly
straight-forward pintation" adding up to "a pintic parable"
about marriage; The Dwarfs, however, was "pintation at
its most pinticular." Darlington summed up his Daily Telegraph review, "Pinter at his most Pinteresque," by blaming
the dialogue rhythm for contributing to a loss of meaning
in the words.

Theatrical criticism of 1963, like earlier years',
continued to be founded upon an assumed and fashionable
Pinter theatre, either lauded or condemned. Critics revealed this most clearly in their objections, as they accused
the author of predictability, pessimism, and non-communication. Even the favorable reviews, however, pointed to this
preconceived world dominated by unchanging themes. For
both detractors and admirers "Pinter" words became increasingly useful. Although there could be no definition of
such terms, the jargon continued to spread. Overall
attitudes of critics towards Pinter corresponded alarmingly
to Smith's warnings: reviewers were becoming trapped in

their own abstractions of the plays.

Scholars, for the most part, also discussed abstractions. Despite a considerable decrease in the volume of writing, their concerns remained essentially unchanged. Only one commentator offered a new approach to the writer. In a Critical Quarterly article, John Russell Brown examined the structures of Pinter's plays. Irrespective of label, Brown wrote, the playwright's work exhibited a characteristic of modern drama: "Exposition has become Development, and Conclusion as well." Such pieces "progressively reveal the inner natures of their characters" by delving to different levels of each character's consciousness.

Other scholars continued the older debate over how to categorize Pinter's work. G. Wilson Knight, although he affixed a new label, described that work in terms of social realism. The power of Pinter's characters came from "below"--"what we call 'instinct' or the 'unconscious mind.' " These lower-class characters brought dignity and force of personality, vitality and nearness to life, as they confronted "the insane paradoxes of a decaying culture." Consequently, Knight identified Pinter as part of a "Kitchen Sink" movement, after the symbol of food, the physical object synonymous with the coarseness of lower-class life.

Martin Esslin, on the other hand, again argued for the Theatre of the Absurd. Although the playwright created realistic dialogue, he had no concern for social questions or political causes; hence, Esslin asserted, Pinter was not a "Kitchen-sink" realist. Because his concern was the communication of a "sense of being" in the modern world, Pinter forced no answers on the situations he presented; rather, he spoke through "extended poetical images." James T. Boulton, likewise, dealt with particular elements--the unknown

and unknowable, the contingency of others, isolation, and the
question of identity--generally considered elements of the Theatre of the Absurd. Boulton saw Pinter's theme as the "terror
of the loneliness of the human situation."

Clearly, scholarship in 1963 revealed little evidence of
progress toward greater understanding of Pinter's art. The
discussion of labels continued while questions of the author's
significance remained unanswered. The fact that scholars un-
questioningly discussed Pinter as a literary subject again indicated his stature and, concomitantly, added to it.

VII

In 1964 Pinter's works received almost constant exposure on both sides of the Atlantic. The Caretaker opened as
a movie (its title changed to The Guest) in New York on January 20 and (title unchanged) in London on March 12. On January 30, the same play opened off-Broadway at the Players
Theatre. In February, the Cambridge Amateur Dramatic Club
performed The Caretaker in London; also in February, The
Collection was done during a one-act play festival at King's
College, London. The commentaries on all of these perfor-
mances were relatively uninspired. New York critics of the
second production of The Caretaker devoted their time chiefly
to comparing the two productions. Although some reviewers
thought the acting and directing of the revival a tour de force,
others felt that because it overemphasized abstractions it remained lifeless. One critic, the Herald Tribune's Judith
Crist, drew attention to an earlier criticism of Pinter's
works: "It is disappointing to discover . . . that on stage

The Caretaker depends almost entirely for its effectiveness on the quality of its performance; the importance and the meaning is not in the lines [sic]."

Reviewers of the movie version, as might be expected, spent most of their effort assessing the effects of the media change. Again, opinions varied radically. Many, like the Newsweek critic and the New Statesman's John Coleman, felt that recapturing the stage play's claustrophobia contributed greatly to the stunning effects of the film. Other critics, Judith Crist of the New York Herald Tribune and Ann Pacey of the London Daily Herald, for examples, disagreed because they thought that the movie's failure to create claustrophobia kept it from measuring up to the stage play.

In addition to these productions, there were three, more important, productions in 1964: The Lover opened (with Beckett's Play) at New York's Cherry Lane Theater on January 4; The Birthday Party, revived by the Royal Shakespeare Company, opened in London on June 18; and The Room and A Slight Ache opened at the Writers Stage Theater in New York on December 9.

The New York reviewers of The Lover added little to the London critics' understanding of the play: most concentrated on the psychological study of marriage relations or on the elements of the Theatre of the Absurd. A number of commentators weighed the relative merits of Pinter's and Beckett's pieces, much as one might compare the pupil's work to the teacher's. The verdicts split fairly evenly: while several praised Pinter for his greater theatricality, others, like Commonweal's Richard Gilman, thought that the shallowness of Pinter's work made him inferior to his master.

Critics most commonly cited shallowness as The

Lover's shortcoming. The combination of wife and mistress,
thought the New York Times' Howard Taubman, is "not a re-
markably fresh idea." Robert Brustein wrote in the New Republic that the play is "a feeble anecdote, only barely rescued
from pure stage trickery."

Again, the phrasing of objections provided ample evidence that a number of critics reacted to the fashionable
Pinterism. Writing in the Herald Tribune, Walter Kerr found
the play's resolution "not surprising" and thought that Pinter
"over-extended his marked talent for polished ambiguity."
Richard Gilman also termed The Lover a weak play, "too
schematic--Pinter's periodic curse."

Six years after the disastrous first production of The
Birthday Party, the play returned to London, fulfilling Hobson's
prophecy. As Philip Hope-Wallace expressed it: "The canon-
isation is complete" for this supposed "modern classic." Although several critics still railed at the play, most now
praised it highly. The criticism, so radically altered in six
years, highlighted the new approaches: either accepting Pinter
as a fashionable major writer, or devaluing his work because
of his familiarity.

Only Jeremy Kingston of Punch offered a new interpretation of the piece. Acknowledging that his was only one of
many possible meanings, Kingston explained the first act as a
kind of birth as Stanley is pulled from the room, the second
act as a living process--Stanley is overwhelmed with guilt and
sins--and the third act, then, as a process of dying. "What
makes [Pinter's] work so exciting," Kingston wrote, "is the
feeling of shapes moving like Krakens beyond the surface of
his play, ordering every move." Most reviewers, however,
merely lauded the play without making any significant

comments on it.

The customary tangents of negative criticism reappeared; most in this case, however, came as reservations within favorable reviews. Two commentators objected to the new production. The Times' critic saw this performance as "slicker and less dangerous" because it indulged in theatrical clichés. Bamber Gascoigne carried the objection further: "Pinter makes it all too obvious" with his overly self-conscious directing.

One critic argued directly against the pressures of the Pinter fashion and criticized the audiences of his plays for making too much of him. Herbert Kretzmer, in his Daily Express review, called the audience a failure for guffawing simply because "it recognised the style [of the play], and felt familiar with it." The playwright, Kretzmer stated, has been "trapped by a vogue" and "has been taken too seriously on the basis of a tiny output."

Other reviewers remained essentially negative about The Birthday Party. Arthur Thirkell of the Daily Mirror, for example, dismissed the play as "a piece of arty-crafty nonsense." J.C. Trewin, continuing his personal vendetta, wrote that while The Birthday Party was "less exasperating" the second time around, this "means simply that we are more conditioned to the theatre of the inexplicit." Trewin still considered it a minor play and Pinter "by no means . . . a major dramatist."

The Birthday Party remained a clearly ascertainable case study in the vicissitudes of Pinter criticism. Although the general character of the reviews was laudatory, reservations and outright condemnations pointed to the constant ambivalence about the playwright's reputation. There had been a profound change towards acceptance of his works over the six

years; yet, here too the negative criticism that had plagued
Pinter remained vocally present.

The Room and A Slight Ache opened off-Broadway to
almost unanimous acclaim. Because these were early Pinter
plays, commentators, in addition to showering adjectives,
looked for recognizable signs of what the playwright's talent
had become in later years. Although most critics agreed that
the pieces were minor, or not fully developed Pinterism, they
discovered such later recurring themes as: the man whose
world is crumbling about him, the gradual disintegration of a
personality, the direct experience of the unnamed, the stagnation of a marriage, the failure of communication, and the
ever-present atmosphere of fear, menace, or dread. Critics,
of course, again concentrated on the "trade-marks" or "hall-
marks" of "Pinter country," such as characters, settings, and
the counterpointing of sound with silence. Favorable reviewers conferred on Pinter such titles as "specialist in fright" and
"Ruler of Enigma," titles which again reflected a supposed
familiarity with the author's idiom. Overall the reaction to
The Room and A Slight Ache demonstrated the usual enthusiastic and indiscriminate attitude of New York reviewers toward
Pinter.

Probably because these are older Pinter works, several
critics raised older objections. One, the Newsweek reviewer,
accused the playwright of obscurity of vision: Pinter was "a
talented playwright who has yet to demonstrate his capacity
for going the imaginative distance." Wilfrid Sheed also
brought out an old complaint in his Commonweal review. He
found both pieces devoid of deeper meanings; though the plays
appeared to be parables or allegories, in the end, Sheed asserted, their symbols "don't add up" to anything.

In contrast to the reviewers' unchanging opinions,

scholars publishing in 1964 offered a number of new perspectives on Pinter. In a Midwest Quarterly article, Florence J.
Goodman demonstrated that The Caretaker presents a picture
of Hell. While Gorky's The Lower Depths shows Hell in social
conditions and O'Neill's The Iceman Cometh shows Hell in self-
delusions--both of which are conditions which may be changed
--Pinter shows that Hell comes from a deeper, lonelier source,
the "human condition itself," which cannot be changed. Ellen
D. Leyburn, writing in Yale Review, described Pinter as part
of a modern theatrical tendency that leads to a loss of "dis-
tinctness" between the traditional categories of tragedy and
comedy. Traditionally, comedy explored "man's weakness"
and tragedy explored man in "boundary situations." However,
Leyburn asserted, now these roles were transposed: men in
the plays of Pinter asked "ultimate questions," and the comedy
served to arouse in the audience a "tragic involvement and the
tragic feelings of pity and terror."

In the New Statesman, Ronald Bryden defined a new
label for Pinter's work--"the Theatre of Situation." His plays
were almost "impromptu" acting situations: "Whatever the
surface dialogue, the situation is battle: domineer or be
domineered, act or be acted off." However, Bryden felt,
creating "memorable characters" was insufficient; "The experiment succeeds, the generalisation from it seems as impossible as ever." Consequently, he noted happily that the
author was moving to greater background, to "the total situation in which real people live and behave," in his later plays.

Other commentators recapitulated earlier views of the
playwright. Ruby Cohn, already discussing "Latter Day"
Pinter plays, saw him concerned with "the ambiguous relationship between appearance and reality." She noted thematic
and situational movements in Pinter's later plays, pointing out

that he was moving away from overt violence, inarticulate characters, and the suffocating room to a menace built around illusions on a "sexual level."

Discussions of the playwright began to appear more frequently in books on theatre history, indicating that pressures of the fashion had made Pinter a figure who must be encountered in contemporary drama. Yet these commentaries, too, reflected earlier statements of reviewers. In his The Theatre of Revolt, Robert Brustein, for example, wrote that Pinter had affinities to those modern playwrights whose work reflected an "existential revolt," in which "the dramatist examines the metaphysical life of man and protests it; existence itself becomes the source of his rebellion." George Sutherland Fraser, although recognizing Pinter's debts to Beckett and Ionesco, praised his "literary quality." Pinter's drama, Fraser wrote in The Modern Writer and His World, was "not of non-communication, but of non-affective communication."

In addition, book discussions of the author reflected earlier objections to his plays. George E. Wellwarth noted, in his The Theatre of Protest and Paradox, traces of Ionesco, Beckett, and Genet in Pinter's work. Wellwarth wrote: "The impression . . . is that of eclectic scholarship rather than of creation." He concluded favorably, nonetheless, calling Pinter "the most promising of England's young playwrights." In The Impossible Theatre, Herbert Blau rephrased complaints about the writer's pessimistic world view. Blau labeled The Birthday Party an "anti-play" because its characters lacked the passion to know the system that victimized them: "It is this positive (nasty word!) side of the victim that one misses in Stanley . . . . "

The recurrence of certain positive and negative arguments in the criticism pointed to a stagnation either in

Pinter's own art or in the assessments of that art. That
some commentators still offered fresh insights indicated that
the latter was the most probable source of stagnation. Production reviews, in particular, demonstrated that the assumption of a rigid pattern in Pinter drama closed the critics'
minds to seeing more than the surface of the plays.

A handful of critics, however, remained aware of this
rigidity on the part of their colleagues. Bryden, in the New
Statesman article mentioned above, perhaps clearly outlined
the problem: "What needs opposing isn't Pinter, but Pinterism and the Pinterites." Those commentators who found it
easy to institutionalize the playwright's form of situational
theatre, Bryden asserted, made it too easy for other writers
to create a superficial popular theatre. Although Bryden was
concerned primarily with the future of dramatic writing, his
observations pointed to the mutual influence of criticism and
creative writing. The picture he painted was dim both for
Pinter and for other dramatists; yet his warnings, as the
warnings of other critics before him, again seemed to go un-
heeded.

                              VIII

There were two productions of new Pinter plays in
1965. The Tea Party, done March 25 on BBC television, received almost unanimous critical acclaim. Most frequently,
reviewers saw it as a portrayal of the psychological disintegration of a self-made man, or as a symbolic war between
the sexes. As expected, they often remarked that Pinter's
idiom and style were here used as brilliantly as usual. Like
Maurice Wiggin of the Sunday Times, who wrote that he now

was getting the "hang of this strange experience of watching a new Pinter play," critics largely expressed their comfort with the playwright's work.

On June 3, 1965, after a two-month warm up tour of the provinces, The Homecoming, Pinter's most recent full-length play, opened in London. Surprisingly, ambivalence and disappointment characterized critical response. Almost all critics, nontheless, praised the production and the author's technical mastery in creating hypnotic dialogue and sharply-etched characters. A number of possible themes were suggested, both by reviewers who liked the play and by those who remained ambivalent: the depths of human degradation; the conflict between those people who operate on things and those who operate in things; the emotional ambiguities within two generations of a family group; the progressive fragmentation of human personality; the endless ambiguity of our perceptions; and the dual nature of woman.

Critics also constructed interpretations around the central character's "homecoming." Some assumed that the homecoming is Teddy's. Stuart Hall, for one, wrote in Encore that the play was a struggle between Teddy and the other members of the family over the possession of Ruth. Teddy loses because he operates on things instead of in them, because he has lost what the family still has: "a grip on life, or, rather, a firm, realistic grip on their own fantasies." Other reviewers saw this conflict as a proletarian struggle against an intellectual, or as a study of animal instincts. Equally often, however, commentators felt Ruth's homecoming the central story and offered interpretations of her actions: a whore's reversion to type, a dissatisfied wife's movement to freedom, and a parable with biblical overtones on her name. The Observer's Penelope Gilliatt noted that in the play "sexual

instinct . . . isn't at all emotional or even physical; it is
practically territorial." Ruth defeats all of the men; " . . .
the moment she has apparently been exploited sexually, she
really has the advantage" because she views her body as
property.

Even in favorable reviews, however, reviewers' ambivalence became clearly evident. Eric Shorter of the Daily
Telegraph, for example, called The Homecoming "gruesomely funny" on its way to "its unedifying conclusion"; and
Penelope Gilliatt thought that through a fault in the author's
"vision," the second half of the play seemed "a shade under-
nourished."

Most objections to the play reflected similar views.
As Gilliatt's comment hinted, many reviewers felt the second
act's ending weak. The Times' critic thought that Pinter had
set out to show a "close family unit, but no such unit takes
shape." Hence, Ruth's staying seemed unmotivated since
she was "not succumbing to the gravitational pull of the
household but merely choosing, for no reason, to stay there."
Anthony Curtis also wrote in the Sunday Telegraph that the
ending of the play failed: " . . . the plunge here into the
erotic has a certain air of desperation about it, redeemed
here only by the comic willingness with which the female is
appropriated."

Commentators most frequently claimed that Pinter's
"vision" fails in The Homecoming. Harold Hobson, though
he praised the play for having no "aesthetic defect," noticed
what he called a "moral vacuum" in the piece. The playwright never commented on the characters or on their fantasies, and Hobson found himself "troubled by [this] complete absence from the play of any moral comment whatso-
ever." Outright critics of The Homecoming also seized upon

this issue.   David Nathan in the Sun noted the usual Pinter
"meal" of violence and sex, and asked: "To what Pinteresque
purpose?"   Writing in the City Press, C.B. Mortlock said
that attempts to discover "some esoteric interpretation" for
the play "will not make its inescapable crudities palatable."
He concluded: "I hope I may never see a nastier play."
The Daily Worker's Jack Sutherland wrote that "the philosophy behind all this is entirely worthless and phoney."   The
author offered "no new flash of illumination in a world preg-
nant with meaninglessness."

Specific comments, in addition to the "Pinteresque"
reference cited above, reflected the customary assumptions
about Pinter.   B.A. Young of the Financial Times called
Pinter's reversal at the end "a brilliant Pinterian stroke."
Jeremy Kingston noticed in his Punch review a "marked
diminution in this play of the mannerisms that have some-
times threatened to lead Mr. Pinter into self-parody."   Odd-
ly, the Times' reviewer criticized Pinter for one of these de-
partures from the expected: the writer breaks one of his
"finest principles"--that "audiences [have] no right to de-
mand indisputable facts about the characters."   In his desire
to provide more background to his characters, Pinter, the
critic felt, tended to dilute the imagination of the audience.

Ironically, although Pinter supposedly remained one of
England's fashionable playwrights and a growing literary
figure, his plays provoked continual controversy over issues
of the utmost importance to any lasting reputation.   Critics
seemed to agree only on his mastery of technique; and some,
in reaction, held even that against him.   Although moral reservations had been raised by earlier commentators, such reservations
about an abstract Pinter vision of the world seemed to become
much more widespread and vociferous over the years.

Only one scholar offered a truly new approach to
Pinter in 1965. Marjorie Thompson, referring particularly
to The Caretaker, discussed Pinter in a Modern Drama
article as one of many dramatists concerned with young people and their predicament in a modern world. These new,
young heroes reacted against the values of materialism, the
nation, and the church, and found themselves in a "state of
eternal muddle," unable to discover their own identities. Yet,
Thompson pointed out, the young, like the old, failed to ac-
complish anything. Despite their efforts, other scholars
seemed to repeat, at least peripherally, ideas of previous
commentators: aspects of the absurd theatre, the quality of
Pinter's realism, the poetic qualities of his dialogue, his
themes of menace and power, and the various aspects of
his style.

Ruby Cohn explained how The Dumb Waiter, like Waiting for Godot, presented "Absurdity" (metaphysical) in
"absurdity" (of worldly dramatic action). In Pinter's dramatization of "man's life on earth," there was no allegory, but
rather a "dialogue between the Absurd, hope, and death."
Repeating earlier ideas, F. J. Bernhard discussed a "supra-
realistic quality" in Pinter's work that transmuted the drab
materials of realism "into something more like poetry than
anything else." Gareth Lloyd Evans, in two short Guardian
articles, also explained how the playwright began with realistic language but, by "driving the familiar towards the
unfamiliar," embodied "something sinister" in his dialogue
and showed "the measure of our defeat as human beings."
Evans asked, "How relevant is Pinter's private hell?" He
concluded that the evidence of The Homecoming, a play without "any centre of meaning," suggested that the author had
become obsessed with "his own 'absurdist' vision of life."

Unless Pinter expanded to a wider world view, Evans wrote,
"Pintermania"might starve.

Other commentators dealt in detail with particular
techniques in Pinter's style. John Russell Brown analyzed
in his "Dialogue in Pinter and Others" how the playwright
constructed his dialogue and used it to portray character.
Brown demonstrated Pinter's use of such techniques as mun-
dane details, almost musical rhythms, jokes and puns,
pauses, silences, and close union of gesture, action and
dialogue. Peter Davison looked at similar techniques. He
explained how "contemporary legitimate drama, " especially
that of Pinter and Beckett, made use of aspects of "popular,
or illegitimate drama--especially music hall, pantomime,
radio, and television." While legitimate forms presupposed
a precise audience reaction--to laugh or to cry--popular
comedy expected the audience to be "multiconscious": "to
apprehend fear and laughter simultaneously, without confusion." Through use of the multiconscious aspect of popular forms, the legitimate drama of Pinter and Beckett created
tension within a "tragic or quasi-tragic framework" and developed a comic-pathetic hero. Lastly, Louis MacNeice
dealt with Pinter's use of parable. Although the author did
not as a rule have "allegorical intentions, " MacNeice wrote
in Varieties of Parable, he often suggested "a whole sheaf of
meanings." By means of a technique of "apparent straightfor-
wardness, " he gave us "what would pass as a dramatic slice
of life and slips in between the lines . . . his recurrent
theme of a cosmic menace."

Two scholars again raised common reservations about
Pinter. In her English Dramatic Form, Muriel C. Bradbrook viewed modern theatre as a "theatre of the dream, "
an experimental exploration of man's inner life. Within

Pinter's work "unfocused feelings of menace, the emergence
of irrational guilt, fear and rage, mask a society in which
the individual is unable to feel much true responsibility, and
therefore little genuine guilt . . . . " Bradbrook, however,
remained critical of the limitations of this view of civilization since "the stimulus must grow ever stronger; the
images . . . allow little variety of response." Joseph
Chiardi, on the other hand, failed to see the cosmic significance in Pinter's plays: "A naturalistic background . . .
militates against the supernatural and against universaliza-
tion." Chiardi also criticized the fashion in his Landmarks
of Contemporary Drama: "A great deal of the mythology
woven by benevolent critics . . . seems to me intellectual
gymnastics. . . . It takes more than these over-simplified
ingredients to make myth."

Despite Evans' prediction, "Pinter-mania" still seemed
healthy. Regardless of the diversity of opinion, Pinter continued to be the subject of more detailed readings and
greater praise of his abilities. Continually he was categor-
ized, pinpointed with labels and philosophies, in hopes that
he would thus be more understandable. Yet counter-trends
continued to grow. Critics spent more and more effort de-
nouncing his plays as shallow, repetitive, and minor. Commentators, likewise, denounced a supposed incompleteness or
pessimism of Pinter's themes, and they forgot that they, not
Pinter, read the abstractions into the plays.

IX

The critical response to the single 1966 production of
Pinter's work followed the customary forms. Critics praised

the October 25 television film of The Caretaker, but despite
their enthusiasm, they made no new or significant comments
on the piece. Most reviewers seemed more concerned with
whether The Caretaker had suffered from the change of
media. Stuart Lane of the Morning Star, the lone negative
critic, repeated the growing reservation about Pinter's work:
"My own search for anything more than technical significance
was unavailing . . . ."

Academic work in 1966, while in many respects also
repetitive, did exhibit some originality. Renee Winegarten
examined Pinter and Shaffer in her article, "The Anglo-
Jewish Dramatist in Search of His Soul." Tracing the Jewish feeling of not belonging in English society, she found
each writer picturing a threatening society and "indulging in
oblique criticism of the shibboleths both of the smaller and
the larger society they know."

In the year that had elapsed since the opening of The
Homecoming, assessing the place of the piece in the Pinter
canon had become a scholarly necessity. Two articles were
devoted solely to this task. In a Tulane Drama Review commentary, Kelly Morris described Pinter as "a poet of the
surface" who creates in The Homecoming "an ingenious com-
position of constricted situational modes--i.e., a comedy of
manners." Morris found no allegory: "The scene itself is
an internally consistent non-specified symbol." Pinter
"builds a poem on family themes," in which he shows "the
bald irony of the family as a civilization-unit" by turning it
into a zoo. Bernard F. Dukore, in his "A Woman's Place,"
examined Ruth's function in this presentation of "the domestic
life of the human animal." Through the "cluster of inter-
woven images: battles for power among human animals,
mating rites, and a dominant wife-mother in a den of sexually

maladjusted males," the playwright creates "a vividly theatrical image of lust and power, and of lust used for power."

Other assessments of Pinter's position in 1966 tended
to repeat earlier comments about his techniques and themes.
Gerald Nelson analyzed the author's use of dialogue to show
"the relation between communication and control." He concluded that Pinter was clearly moving away from Ionesco and
Beckett because he remained involved with his characters
"as individual human beings," not merely as symbols.
Richard Schechner wrote that "the essential characteristic
of Pinter's work is its conceptual incompleteness." While
the surface structure was complete, "the 'conceptual world'
out of which the plays emerge, is sparse, fragmented." A
truly disinterested artist, Pinter explored "the mechanics of
his art." His question, "what can the theatre do?", led him
to create the illusion of a real world in which he posited
"real questions without suggesting real answers." Kent G.
Gallagher, on the other hand, examined Caretaker to see how
the playwright achieved "the remarkable and striking, the unusual and bizarre." Gallagher then discussed a number of
"dramaturgical distortions": "hyper-realism"; "disjointed
stichomythia"; "long incongruous speeches"; "fast and loose
. . . symbolism"; and "pseudo-symbols"--objects that appear to function as symbols but do not.

Two scholars studied Pinter as a member of the
Theatre of the Absurd. Alberta E. Feynman wrote that the
non-characters in absurd plays "are fetal in nature. They
have not yet achieved humanity." While other writers seemed
to be moving away from such characters, Feynman observed,
"only Harold Pinter still seems able consistently to devise
full-length dramas peopled with fetal beings--plays in which
life is still equated to trauma, and birth is still equated to

death." Clyde G. Smallwood, on the other hand, combed plays by absurd dramatists for basic concepts of Existentialism. Looking at two Pinter plays, Smallwood discovered several ideas. In The Birthday Party he found expressions of the instability and the contingency of the human being, and in The Room, the instability and the bounding-leap of the human being. Smallwood concluded that Pinter used these concepts "to point up the difficulty of the human being to establish an effective community."

Discussing The Caretaker in The Present Stage, John Kershaw seemed to review almost all of the concerns commentators had thus far had with Pinter's art. Although Kershaw identified Pinter as an "Absurd" writer, he admitted that the author's primary concern was drama, not presenting "the basic problems of our time." First, Kershaw praised Pinter's dialogue: as "poetic" since the words had levels of meaning; as extraordinarily "organic" in quality since it advanced the play and gave insight into the characters; and as "so carefully and perceptively organised [that] it is more convincingly real than real dialogue." Kershaw then lauded the deep psychological characterization as a second achievement in The Caretaker. Lastly, Kershaw examined Pinter's vision of reality. The playwright dealt thematically with characters faced by "the primary basic problem of being," the "time when reality must be faced; and reality is not the world outside the self, it is the self." By disposing of old dramatic categories, Pinter approached "an interpretation of reality which has certainly as much if not more validity than most 'realist' drama."

Certain catchwords continually recurred: realism, absurd, hyper-realism, realistic dialogue, poetic dialogue, psychological realism, power struggles, communication and

non-communication, incompleteness--all variously attempts to
define the fashionable "Pinteresque" abstraction. While focal
points remained static and conclusions shifted only slightly,
implicitly assumed by now in almost all of these essays was
Pinter's literary greatness.

X

     Broadway saw two major productions of Pinter's works
in 1967: The Homecoming opened on January 5 at the Music
Box, and The Birthday Party opened on October 3 at the Booth.
In London, a new Pinter one-act, The Basement, was shown
February 20 on BBC television.
     The New York critics' reactions to The Homecoming
differed somewhat from the reactions of London critics in
1965. New York reviewers tended to see it as a black
comedy, which to some extent countered possible moral objections. More of them responded favorably to the play, although few could avoid expressing some reservations. Again,
the critics overwhelmingly acknowledged Pinter's technical
virtuosity.
     The thematic interpretations they offered reflected
earlier readings: the relationships between sex, violence
and power; a criticism of human degradation; a mythic study
of blood consciousness; a subconscious struggle for self-
preservation; a parable of the death of values; a satire on
domesticity; and an outrageous sex farce. A number of reviewers suggested that The Homecoming represented a night-
marish dream. In the Reporter, Derek Morgan wrote that it
was a dream on an abstract level in Teddy's mind: "The
whole play may well be a bad dream he is having one restless

night back there 'on the old campus.'" Whitney Bolton of
the Morning Telegraph also saw the play dealing with a
man's dream of seeing his wife violated: "In his case, reality, not a dream is experienced."

A noticeable development in the criticism of this production was the vehement dialogue over the motivations of
the play's characters. While London critics, for the most
part, expressed bafflement at their behavior, New York
critics divided fairly equally: some repeating the earlier
complaints, and others, in a large sense reflecting scholarly commentaries on the work, offering theories to show that
the characters' actions were both necessary and proper.

The reviewers' repugnance again led to many of the
objections. Robert Brustein, for one, felt that Pinter "tends
to exploit the bizarre too much entirely for its own sake."
Vogue critic, Anthony West, rebuked the author for writing
a piece that almost totally lacked "meaning and dramatic
interest." The play, which West saw as being about
"woman's fall," failed because it "revolves upon a dim
crisis in the life of a mediocre spirit"--Ruth, who is "one
of those dopy girls for whom nothing can be done, and about
whom there is little to be said." Similarly, Commentary's
Jack Richardson felt that since the playwright attempted to
show people, he had to present convincing motivations: viewers had to be convinced "that [the characters'] inconsistent
antics are more than lunatic meanderings or the results of a
self-indulgent dramatic style."

Other reviewers attempted to counter such objections
by explaining what they thought the author did in the play.
Walter Kerr, in two New York Times articles, wrote that
Pinter wanted to contradict our attempts to deal with the
world logically and rationally: "The world might go another

way--a surprising and ultimately unexplained way--if it went
its own way, indifferent to philosophies." The playwright's
theory worked in the final third of the play, "forcing us to
accept the unpredictable as though it were the natural shape
of things." Richard Gilman in Newsweek explained The Homecoming as a movement from a realistic vision of "domestic
horror" to a ritual and mythic encounter between the contrary
fantasies of the characters. The ritual carried the characters "beyond morality"; they acted rightly within "the terms
and conditions of the play." In Christian Century, Robert G.
Kemper turned to the ideas of the Theatre of the Absurd.
By upsetting our normal experience of reality, he wrote, the
play shocked us to a new picture of man as either amoral or
evil, without creative redeeming qualities. Hence, The Homecoming had "little 'action' but plenty of 'absurd' situations."

     To explain Pinter's logic, other critics fell back upon
an assumed Pinteresque form. Alan S. Downer, for one,
wrote in the Quarterly Journal of Speech: "The play is the
expected mixture of irrelevant exposition, portentous pause,
and off-stage violence that the audience has been trained to
respect in Harold Pinter's work." Pinter creates a world of
"pure theatre" that is "apart from all the concerns of society," and he "invites the audience to make of it what they
will."

     Negative criticism of The Homecoming spanned the
usual range. Walter Kerr accused the playwright of "drain-
ing away our interest with his deliberate delay." Pinter,
he wrote, attempted to write a full-length play, using no more
material than he would for a one-act play. Several critics
concurred. The Morning Telegraph's Whitney Bolton felt the
play "uncommon long [sic] and often tedious in its development"; and Hudson Review's John Simon wrote that although

Pinter could write good short plays, when he wrote longer
ones, he reverted to "desperate stratagems . . . to keep the
scales from tipping over into total meaninglessness . . . ."
Concomitantly, a common objection to the play was that the
author merely played tricks, and was deliberately vague and
repetitious. Richard Watts of the Post said that in the end
"you suspect that [he] has been something of a trickster."
Robert Brustein accused Pinter of giving in to "a vaguely
vulgar streak of theatricality." Of course, at least one
critic, Arthur Cavanaugh, writing in Sign, failed to see any
"significance and hidden statements about Life Today" in the
"sordid" play.

Because of these reservations and perhaps other un-
voiced ones, many reviewers believed The Homecoming not up
to Pinter's best level of work. While a number made such
comparisons, they generally remained as ambivalent as
Richard Watts, who commented: "The Homecoming is less
than first-rate Harold Pinter, but it proves that even Pinter
not at the peak of his skill can be more exciting than most
contemporary playwrights in their top form."

Despite such ambivalence, The Homecoming continued
to be a focus of attention. The writer of a New York Times
article asked seven prominent figures, ranging from writers
to clergymen, "What's Pinter up to?" and received widely
differing answers. The Times also published letters and
poems on the play a number of times. Later in the spring,
The Homecoming was voted the best play of the 1966-67 theatrical season. In a Saturday Review article, Henry Hewes
listed The Homecoming's achievements: "Most fully realized
theater work"; "Best serious play"; "Most indelible theater
experience"; "Best director (serious play: Peter Hall)"; and
"Best male lead performance (serious play: Paul Rogers)."

The only explanation why so relatively few New York critics had moral objections to the brutal aspects of the play was that most of them, unlike their London counterparts, either saw the play on an allegorical level that dictated an independent, non-realistic logic, or, regardless of whether they found any meaning, saw it as a black comedy.

The contrast between the reactions to the London and New York productions of The Homecoming again indicated both the flourishing Pinter fashion and the deep-seated controversies about his art. Two Broadway reviewers felt it necessary to comment on the reactions of their colleagues. John Simon chastised both the playwright and his critics: the former for saying nothing, and the latter for falling all over themselves to discover meanings in his plays. Glenn Loney, writing in Educational Theatre Journal, expressed more sympathy for Pinter. He wrote that it had become "the height of fashion to bore one's friends with endless analyses of the allegorical functions of The Homecoming." Critics apparently needed to make the terms of the piece correspond to their own terms before they could find meaning in it; consequently, Loney asserted, "what emerges from much of this is not always insight into the play but into the critic." Again, however, the majority of commentators ignored such warnings, as their reactions to The Homecoming over two years clearly showed. Their endlessly refined interpretations, their dialogue over Pinter's characterization and techniques, and their reactions of moral repugnance all cumulatively offered little more than massive confusion, severe impediments to experiencing the play on the stage. Ironically, as the letters to the New York Times demonstrated, the fashion became contagious.

The reviewers of the BBC television production of

The Basement offered mixed responses and few innovations.
For so slight an output, however, the similarities to earlier
criticism were striking. Kenneth Eastaugh of the Daily
Mirror wrote that "a Pinter below par still has that sure
touch of genius." Before offering his reading, he noted that
this piece was simple to understand by "Pinter standards."
Sylvia Clayton was less complimentary. She wrote in her
Daily Telegraph review: "as usual in a Pinter play, the man
in possession was mesmerised into yielding his territory to
a powerful intruder." But she felt that "in this ornate, self-
indulgent play the author's devices did not create tension or
magic." In the Sunday Telegraph, Philip Purser praised the
playwright's skill in creating images and in using the television medium, but he asked finally: ". . . to what end?
When the flattery of the eye was over, what remained to
occupy the mind?" Such commentary again revealed the
stagnation in Pinter criticism.

The response to the New York production of The
Birthday Party provided additional evidence that the fashion
remained strong and stifling. Compared to the reactions to
the 1964 London production, the Broadway reactions exhibited
the logical culmination of critics' adjustments to the work.
The praise became extremely lavish; the dissenting comments
far less in number and importance. Unlike their earlier
response to The Homecoming, Broadway reviewers of The
Birthday Party expressed no ambivalence or negativism. On
the other hand, they offered no profound, or even original,
insights into Pinter's art. Though their praise became almost unanimous, they seldom went beyond vague raptures.
Again the responses seemed to point to a rigid sterility in
thought about the author.

Most reviewers gave only loud applause. For the

Times' Clive Barnes, The Birthday Party was "a new kind of
heroic drama," dealing with modern anxieties and reaching
the "heights of poetic apostrophe." Martin Gottfried of
Women's Wear Daily saw the play as "proof enough of
Pinter's status as an artist valid beyond time, transient material and passing fancies." Not to be outdone, Edward Sothern
Hipp in the Newark Evening News lauded the piece as a
"tantalizingly inexplicit" black comedy, an "exploration of
various human minds." He noted favorably that "Pinterism
takes over," and he praised the "Pinteresque" dialogue.
Harold Clurman contended that the play was "not obscure."
He visualized a "parable" of Death's agents coming to claim
the play's "anti-hero," who has been reduced to "a menaced
and quivering atom in a senseless, horribly vacuous world."

Some reviewers, though disliking the play as a whole,
still praised the author for the sharp characterization. Only
the critic for Variety gave full expression to his reservations
about The Birthday Party. At the same time, he echoed
what a number of earlier critics had noted: "For Pinter
faddists, all this will be richly meaningful and significant.
To the non-dedicated, however, it may seem exasperatingly
slow and cryptic, if not dull." Reviewers also variously
pointed to obscurity of character motivation, lack of under-
lying substance, and failure to have cosmic significance as
shortcomings of the work.

Again the "vogue" entered clearly. Even Walter Kerr,
though he made the most detailed assessment of the play,
fell into the trap, as he referred to "Pinteresque effects"
and to "Pinterites," of which he considered himself one.
Richard Gilman called The Birthday Party "so much manner
and so little style," almost, in retrospect, a parody of
Pinter's own later work. Christian Century's critic, Lowell

D. Streiker, called the play "excellent Pinterism." He
wrote, however: "Pinterism, which may be defined as total
indifference to just such questions [of personality, situation,
guilt and resolution] by its very essence judges itself to be
unsatisfactory."

For all of the positive reaction to The Birthday Party
generally, the reviewers brought out little that was original
or insightful. The playwright's name instantly prompted
most critics to whole-hearted praise. As Richard Gilman
pointed out, critics seemed to want to make the play greater
than it is because Pinter turned out so great: "because he
is so much now he could not have been so much less then."

In sheer bulk, 1967 brought the largest output of
academic writing about Pinter to date. Numerous articles
either dealt with the entire Pinter canon or with particular
plays and techniques. In addition, the playwright was for
the first time the subject of two extended treatments: Walter
Kerr's long essay in the Columbia University series on
modern writers, and Arnold P. Hinchliffe's book-length
survey in the Twayne English Authors series. Despite the
great volume, commentators approaching Pinter from new
perspectives remained outnumbered by those repeating earlier
approaches.

A handful of scholars made significant points about
individual plays. Stephen Prickett, for one, discussed The
Caretaker as one of a number of modern plays moving away
from the naturalistic sequence of speech and action. The
playwright, Prickett wrote, employed two particular techniques: "ritual," a series of formal actions of symbolic
import used to express inarticulate thoughts and feelings,
and "Phatic Communion," speech used "not to express ideas,
but to express communal solidarity . . . through other

apparently random and meaningless topics." Palmer Bovie,
for another, approached The Lover as one in a long series
of treatments of the Amphitryon seduction theme. In showing the "inexhaustible life" of the myth, Pinter reduced the
theme to absurdity and substituted sex for the deus ex
machina as he showed the couple's search for "the lusty re-
newal of their love."

Alrene Sykes examined The Dwarfs, attempting to
decipher the identity of the title figures. She noted that
their appearances seemed to be linked to "the disintegration
of the relationships between Len and his two friends." Sykes
theorized: "Is it possible that these dwarfs represent, not
the poetic imagination, and not the unseen rulers of the
world, but simply the miseries, jealousies, and ignoble-
nesses of the dissolving relationship, ending when the relationship itself ends, leaving Len in the antiseptic state of
dead emotions?" In connection with a campus production of
A Slight Ache, the University of Illinois Department of English published three brief essays on the play in a special
publication, Midwest Monographs. In one essay Neil Kleinman analyzed Edward as "a composite of the Enlightenment
Man" who attempted always to name names, to qualify the
world, thereby hoping to understand it. The descriptive
names that Edward provided paradoxically led to a more
chaotic and mysterious reality, to new fears. Pinter showed
us, Kleinman wrote, that "we cannot avoid experiencing the
unnamable." In a second article, Richard Wasson pointed
to the movement in modern drama away from plots and
rhythms of tragedy and comedy toward the genre of mime:
"the direct presentation of all-too-human man acting in a
silent nature." Pinter, however, moved the mime structure,
which normally makes no judgments, "toward the confirma-

tion of the world of fantasy." He used his drama, then,
to project "a recurrent dream in which the male finds himself victimized . . . by the female, who finally projects her
fantasy on mute reality."

Many interpretations of individual plays, however,
were merely restatements of earlier positions. Daniel
Curley, in the same issue of Midwest Monographs, discussed
a more familiar topic: what he called the "intruder-woman
complex," through which Pinter showed "the failure of male
potency as the cause of female aggressiveness." Richard
Gilman in a New York Times article assessed The Homecoming as the culminating work in the author's movement
toward a new kind of "realism." In the characters, Pinter
presented "archetypes of being, warring with one another,"
and ultimately, "the property of consciousness" lost decisive-
ly to "the absolutism of the physical self." In a Saturday
Review article, Abraham N. Franzblau, a psychiatrist who
had offered an interpretation of The Birthday Party, turned
turned his attention to The Homecoming. He wrote that the
concern of the piece was "ménage-à-trois, a powerful unconscious attraction [existing] between two men . . . who
make love to the same woman in each other's presence."
Lastly, David Cook and Harold F. Brooks saw The Caretaker as a "tragic farce" in which the central theme was "the
fear of exposure . . . , the fear of being known too closely
by other people."

Other commentators, while offering interpretations of
the entire Pinter canon, also tended to restate previous insights. Augusta Walker found two types of subject matter in
the playwright's work: "one, the little allegory about life,
death and cosmic concepts; the other, the undercurrents and
drives in human relationships," both of which point to "our

lostness from cause and origin and our inability to maintain
creature associations with each other." John Pesta saw the
"precariousness of man's existential security" as the unifying
theme in Pinter's work. Through use of the "usurper"
Pinter indicated "that men are prevented from reaching re-
warding relationships, wherein the truest security lies, by
their own selfishness, pride, or weakness." R.F. Storch,
on the other hand, thought the author's use of "the running
away from certain family situations" a major unifying agent.
Storch pointed primarily to the ambivalence that Pinter created as he showed "the middle-class family, both as shelter-
ing home longed for and dreamed of, and as many-tentacled
monster strangling its victim."

Several scholars again brought out existential, or
absurd, interpretations of Pinter. In his Harold Pinter,
Walter Kerr saw the playwright as "the only man working in
the theater today who writes existentialist plays existential-
ly." Rather than being restatements of existentialist themes,
his plays functioned according to the "existentialist sequence":
"existence precedes essence." His characters developed
without the limitations of preconception; they groped for their
own identities. Arnold P. Hinchliffe asserted in his Harold
Pinter, one of the most thorough treatments of the author
thus far, that Pinter was "quintessentially the English . . .
representative of Absurd Theater." Hinchliffe then dealt
with each play individually, demonstrating the development
of Pinter's "ability to fuse European Absurdity with the
English way of life, the foreign with the native, the time-
less and the universal with the immediate and local." This
ability gave the plays "a lasting quality" that enabled Hinchliffe to assert that the playwright "will remain one of
Britain's most important twentieth-century dramatists--in my

opinion, the most important."

One commentator, Charles Marowitz, even employed
the term "Pinterism" as he surveyed the playwright's work
in a New York Times article. In this case, defining the
term became the central key to understanding Pinter. Yet,
Marowitz finally offered no new interpretations and resorted
to metaphors: "A Pinter play is always an x-ray touched up
to suggest it is a snapshot, and its details reveal the desperate struggle of the organism to eject deadly bacteria."

Two scholars also vented the usual objections in their
studies of Pinter. Victor E. Amend, after discussing the
author's "credits," pointed out that he seemed to be exhaust-
ing his subject matter through repetitions from play to play.
Amend listed five major objections: (1) failure of symbolism
under close analysis, (2) too many ambiguities, (3) repetition
of the failure of communication as a subject, (4) characters
with "grubby souls," and (5) a "negative approach to values."
All of these "debits," Amend wrote, stemmed from the limitations of overrepetition and kept Pinter, while a good writer,
from having a "quality of greatness." In his New Trends in
Twentieth Century Drama, Frederick Lumley also criticized
the dramatist, in this case for things that many other commentators had lauded. Lumley thought Pinter's world "an
incomplete one, his characters . . . expressly without
qualities, his plays without a philosophy or the levels of
communication which are essential if his drama is to have
universal validity." Lumley held against Pinter the lack of
social or abstract message and the use of "intuition" as a
unifying thread. In fact, Lumley characterized "Pinterism"
by its "pure improvisation of situations, creating characters
out of the minimum of information, reacting to the milieu
they belonged." The playwright's theatre of instant intuition,

Lumley concluded, failed to create memorable characters
or to stimulate ideas: "an instant theatre does not last, nor
is intuition the same as imagination."

Almost over-abundant enthusiasm was the overall
characteristic of commentaries on Pinter in 1967. Reviews
of productions witnessed the constancy of his popularity, and
as several reviewers continued to warn, in some instances
critics reacted more to the enthusiasm than to the actual
play. The volume of academic writing indicated the dramatist's growing literary status. The undercurrents, however,
still highlighted the unresolved issues that must affect
Pinter's final stature in British drama. Dissenting critics
pointed to his ambiguity or, as some of them expressed it,
his failure to say anything; his debts to the continental avant-
garde, through which they implied a lack of originality; his
dehumanized characterizations; and the possibility of repetition in his techniques and themes. Although most commentators seemed to feel that these issues were no longer in
doubt, a significant number of responsible critics raised
these questions for each of Pinter's new plays. Both pro-
ponents and opponents failed to remember Esslin's warning:
a few years and a handful of plays could not provide ade-
quate perspective.

Though particular facets of the Pinter fashion changed,
the writer still remained trapped. As the defining term of
a supposed movement failed, commentators coined a new
term and forced it upon him. Thus, while any critic might
feel comfortable with a particular term, there seemed to be
a progression: from menace, to realism and absurd, to
hyper-realism, and finally to Pinterism. Yet such "development" in the criticism could be no more than an illusion
since each term represented an attempt to define

categorically something impossible to define.   Although the
idea of an abstract Pinterism had plagued the criticism
repeatedly, now it had become the dominant term defining
the fashion.

XI

Pinter's works were produced a great many times in
1968 and 1969.   The Public Broadcast Lab performed The
Dwarfs on United States television January 28, 1968; the
BBC broadcasted a new play, Landscape, on radio April 25
and May 12, 1968; and two plays originally done on British
television, The Tea Party and The Basement, opened off-
Broadway on October 15, 1968.   In addition, on December
9, 1968, The Birthday Party opened in New York as a
movie; and the one-act plays, Landscape and Silence, opened
in London July 2, 1969.

Daily News' reviewer, Ben Gross, offered the only
new comment on the television production of The Dwarfs; he
noticed "a marked homosexual element," but did not
elaborate on the idea.   The other critics, for the most part,
discussed allegories that had been detailed before.

Reviews of the radio production of Landscape were
almost uniformly enthusiastic.   The reviewers lauded what
they saw as new developments in Pinter's art.   Peter Lewis
of the London Daily Mail praised the author's "delicate"
writing as he created a play "refined to the slenderest
skeleton."   The Times' critic also saw this change; he
called the character Beth "utterly different" from "a traditional Pinter character."   In the piece, the playwright
used "another style of writing," and the critic's explanation

complemented that of Lewis: "The phraseology has its
familiar exactitude, but it has besides a fresh and excep-
tionally limpid quality. From it emerges the portrait of a
woman drawn with a tenderness that reveals in the author a
new poetic, even romantic strain." Only one critic, Paul
Bailey of the Listener, disliked Landscape, and he objected
chiefly to that same style, which he parodied: "It was a
strange play, Short and strange. Not quite the usual Pinter.
Not quite. No games . . . . Not so much gratuitous violence as usual. No, not so slick, It was more like Beckett,
Like Play. Not so good. It couldn't be. Beckett is an
original. Pinter isn't. Whatever they say."

    The reactions to the New York production of The Tea
Party and The Basement were more substantial and brought
out the usual range of comments. The response demonstrated
the static condition of Pinter criticism. Although most reviewers called the latter play markedly inferior, they almost
unanimously praised the evening's fare. Again, few of them
found new experiences in the playwright's art. The majority
reacted to the pieces as Whitney Bolton did in his Morning
Telegraph review: they "[tell] us that females can exert
a terrible magic and an equally terrible fate on defenseless
males." Or they approached The Tea Party in particular as
the Newark Evening News' Daphne Kraft did: the story of a
man's becoming "completely isolated when he is thrown up
against the fact that he, and those of his family and office,
do not behave as rational and logical machines." Only
Harold Clurman differed somewhat when he summed up the
major theme: "Most of Pinter's work comes to this: bereft
of all but a residual animal instinct and no firm moral or
intellectual objectives, man loses his human identity."

    Despite their compliments, many critics considered

the plays below par for the author, and yet they managed to
excuse his failings. The Post's Richard Watts, Jr., for
example, wrote that though The Tea Party and The Basement
are not "top category" Pinter, "they leave no doubt that they
are the work of a notable, if perversely cryptic dramatic in-
telligence." Clive Barnes of the New York Times thought
that although the plays were "to some extent . . . minor
Pinter," they were still "better than major almost anyone
else." In the New Yorker review, Edith Oliver repeated the
same sentiments in similar words. Richard P. Cooke, however, made no excuses in the Wall Street Journal: ". . . this
is not Pinter at his best. If the plays did not bear the
author's name I doubt they would cause much of a stir." His
comment perhaps offered a valid perspective on the operation
of the theatrical fashion.

Critics made many statements based on the preconcep-
ceptions of Pinter characters, plots, and atmosphere.
Several again accused the dramatist of self-parody. Most
often, as in the case of Walter Kerr, reviewers directed
this complaint solely at The Basement. Kerr wrote in his
Times review that "it is as though Pinter had snapped on his
electric typewriter and let the machine do the play out of
memory." The Variety critic, however, applied the objection
to both plays, "clearly open to the charge of being 'Pinterish. '"

When the film version of The Birthday Party opened
on December 9, 1968, the reviews mirrored those of the
earlier Pinter movie. Reviewers either praised the film
highly for the mood it created, despite its obscurity; or they
panned it as an intellectual exercise that failed to communicate with the audience. Most often, however, they analyzed
the effects of the change from play to movie. Vincent Canby

wrote in the New York Times that the film was a "good
recording of an extraordinary play." The Morning Telegraph's Leo Mishkin, likewise, though he found the movie
"just as cryptic . . . and just as puzzling" as the stage
version, acknowledged that the former's close-ups enabled
it to create "more terror." The Variety reviewer, however,
objected to the director's use of close-ups and to his camera
tracking because he felt that these techniques impeded com-
prehension of the dialogue.

When the two most recent Pinter pieces, Landscape
and Silence, opened July 2, 1969, at the Aldwych, critics
surprisingly regressed to the strong negativism of their reactions to Pinter's earliest works. The two short plays
seemed to mark a change in his style and themes, as noted
by the earlier reviewers of Landscape. Now, however, the
commentators divided: a few critics claiming that the plays
witnessed new poetic heights for the author, and the majority
asserting that the pieces detracted from Pinterism. Generally, reviewers saw the theme as isolation. As Frank Marcus
wrote in the Sunday Telegraph: "They are studies of loneliness: memory plays illustrating man's isolation." The
Sunday Times' Harold Hobson, from a different angle, saw
Pinter saying that "what is important is not the past, but
the continuing influence that this past exercises on the
present . . . . "

Reviewers most often saw the texture of the dialogue
as poetic, and they had mixed reactions to this quality.
Irving Wardle, although he found Silence incomprehensible,
wrote in the Times that the interweaving of dialogue in
Landscape was "elegiac mosaic"; and he concluded that the
piece was "a theatrical poem to which poetic rather than
stage criteria apply." The Daily Telegraph's John Barber

made a similar point as an objection: "[they] are almost
too densely textured for immediate theatrical effect." B.A.
Young of the Financial Times was more negative. He found
Silence a poem and "not a play at all." Pinter "has taken
the scheme further into poetry and away from reality."

Young also noticed Pinter's new stylistic similarities
to Beckett, and as most of the reviewers did, he thought the
change ineffective. Though Pinter had in Silence arrived at
"Beckett country," Young called this a "sterile promontory."
In Plays and Players, Robert Cushman made the same comparison and concluded that Pinter did not have "anything like
his master's formal skill, nor his instinct for the crushing,
inevitable symbol."

Only a handful of reviewers viewed the new style,
and the plays, favorably. Harold Hobson, continuing to
champion Pinter, wrote that were the author an unknown,
"either [play] would be sufficient to establish his reputation
as a dramatist of the highest, subtlest class." Frank
Marcus concluded that "in the context of current avant-garde
practice, [Pinter] is also something of a revolutionary: by
which I mean that he remains uniquely and unmistakably
himself."

Commentators more often reacted negatively to the
style and the plays. The Evening Standard's Milton Shulman,
for example, disliked Pinter's move towards "minimal
drama": "Written by anyone else, I doubt if these plays
would ever have been considered seriously by the Royal
Shakespeare Co. . . . ." J.W. Lambert, likewise, noted
"a marked shrinkage of scale" in Landscape and Silence.
Several critics did not recognize changes in Pinter's style.
Barry Norman of the Daily Mail called both plays "an ex-
hibition by Harold Pinter of running on the spot," of "getting

nowhere in great style." Norman wrote that "we've been through this bit before." Similarly, J.C. Trewin accused the author of "parodying himself." Just as he had always done, Trewin wrote that both pieces were definitely minor and "would become soporific if it were not for the prestige of [Pinter's] name."

More serious negative criticism came from two critics, whose comments also highlighted the sudden disenchantment with Pinter. In the New Statesman Benedict Nightingale accused the playwright of creating plays that "[lack] depth": "It's certainly true that what looks like depth in his work is simply an awareness of complexities he doesn't choose to investigate." He "has nothing new to say: he is simply saying the old things more starkly," and Nightingale asked: "shall we . . . have something substantial from the man himself before long?" Similarly, Catholic World's reviewer, Catharine Hughes, commented that Pinter's characters' "refusal to make contact has been carried to its farthest extreme thus far" in the new works. Such a course, she warned, might be "limited" and "risky" since his plays thus became "obviously less inherently dramatic."

The majority of the critics of this recent production expressed ambivalence, or outright dissatisfaction. Positive statements, especially on Silence, were few, and they contributed little to an understanding of the plays. Though many critics recognized a change in the author's art, they often found the change sterile and unoriginal. Those reviewers who saw a stagnation attributed the fault primarily to the playwright. Whether the reactions to Landscape and Silence marked a significant change in the trends of Pinter criticism, or whether the responses merely demonstrated a temporary vacillation of fashion, cannot yet be known. Nonetheless,

Pinter here strongly encountered the limitations of fashion: reviewers, holding preconceptions about Pinterism, thought it stagnating; yet they remained unreceptive to changes in Pinter's creative work.

The volume of scholarly writing on Pinter decreased somewhat in 1968 and 1969. Indicative of his current appeal as a literary subject, however, in addition to numerous articles scholars published three more book-length studies and a bibliography of scholarly material about him. Again, for the most part, commentators addressed the same problems of theme, character, and technique and arrived at much the same conclusions. The few interesting ideas resulted from approaching older material from different angles, or from applying older theories to new plays. In particular, The Homecoming and Landscape became the subjects of extensive scholarly attention. Other scholars, of course, continued to hunt through the entire Pinter canon for continuities or developments.

Among fresh treatments of the author were two articles by John Lahr. In "Pinter the Spaceman" Lahr examined primarily The Homecoming and Landscape to show that a Pinter play is like a modern sculpture, an object in space: "Objects in space are dramatic; man's reaction to them is theater." By cutting-out normal theatrical conventions, the playwright focused the audience's attention on the stage moment itself, leading to a sense of "immediacy." In a later article, "The Language of Silence," Lahr further explored the idea of the "moment" in Pinter's art as he examined the author's use of silence as "an articulate energy which gives resonance to the spoken word." Silence focused attention on the mysteries of the "living and unpredictable present" and, at the same time, enabled words to "become,

once again, insinuating symbols." Ultimately, Lahr asserted, the silences reflected a "primal silence--the word which
came with man as he emerged from Eden, sinful, conscious
of his vulnerability, longing to cloak himself."

Katherine Burkman, on the other hand, saw Pinter's
plays founded on ritual. She interpreted A Slight Ache in
the light of ancient fertility rites and demonstrated that the
action of the play closely followed a ritual pattern: the
sacrifice of the god-king (Edward) representing winter, followed by the resurrection or coming of the new god of spring
or summer (the Matchseller), concluded by marriage to the
earth-mother or fertility goddess (Flora). Yet the author,
Burkman asserted, did raise some new and "haunting" questions; when he represented the new summer god as "ugly,
smelly, and passive," he seemed to present a truly "tragicomic" picture. In her dissertation, Burkman expanded this
approach to include more of the plays. She found two types
of ritual: daily habitual activities which tended to be empty
of meaning, and sacrificial rites which forced the characters
away from the daily rituals into a new awareness of life.

Likewise, Arnold P. Hinchliffe, seeking to show an
organic pattern in the later plays, offered a new insight in
his article, "Mr. Pinter's Belinda." The pattern Hinchliffe
discovered revolved around sexual matters: the view of a
woman as wife/mother/mistress/whore. As the attitudes
towards these roles were explored in successive plays, the
characters gradually realized these roles were desirable.
The Homecoming, Hinchliffe concluded, "is the end of
Pinter's investigation of the sexual matter." Here, in the
character of Ruth, the goddess and flirt and the wife/mother/
whore roles are seen as naturally together.

Bert O. States saw Pinter's art as one which was

"shifting its focus from an attention to the content for its own sake (our Absurd 'condition') to the interesting symmetries inherent in it." The dramatist maintained an ironic detachment from the stage happenings. His characters also engaged in this ironic struggle: irony became a game of one-up-manship with each character trying to reach a "triumph of perspective" on the situation.

Lastly, Hugh Nelson, in his "The Homecoming: Kith and Kin," advanced the most extensive treatment of the play thus far. Nelson saw the play as "structurally a very traditional piece of playwrighting," in which the exposition revealed a family situation "unbalanced, out of phase." The central movement, or development, "is Ruth's process of self-discovery." Since Pinter's vision of human relationships was basically "dialectical," the resolution of the play "is not to be taken as final" although it had resolved one set of contradictions. Nelson demonstrated that Ruth's movement was toward becoming both "Kith" and "Kin," toward being both known by and related to Teddy's family. Yet, in the end, the playwright revealed in the examples of Max and Lenny that the family values were false: "Beneath the stated values of the play, there is a total absence of values, a void which is filled by the human family's animal struggle to survive and perpetuate itself."

Although even the 1968-1969 articles discussed thus far were to some degree a differently-angled slice of what had been said earlier about the author, the remaining academic work for this period lacked even this distinction. John Lahr in yet another article saw Pinter's work as a "supra-realism," similar to Chekhov's, that without prejudgment showed the "mute isolation between Man and object." Percy C. Dillon examined his plays for

characteristics of the French Theatre of the Absurd. Gerald
Mast offered an interpretation of The Homecoming's characters that showed that consistent personalities "absolutely
determine" the action, making it "not only credible but
necessary." Peter C. Thornton discussed three early plays
to show that "blindness, represented more and more allusive-
ly from play to play, [proves] to be a dominant and effective
symbol of the confrontation with death, physical or spiritual."
Discussing the three full-length plays, Earl J. Dias demonstrated recurring themes--the battle for dominance and the
condemnation of society's "fundamental hypocrisy"--that contributed to the "world" of Pinter. Ray Orley examined types
of menace in the author's works to show: "Dramatically, as
well as politically, terror and menace are most essential
elements of Harold Pinter's vision of life: the horror of
existence presented in truly threatening and frightening
terms."

The three book-length studies also tended to sound
repetitive. In his Harold Pinter, Ronald Hayman surveyed
the dramatist's plays and examined changes in his style as
it gained in subtlety and changes in his thematic treatments
of "the safety of the womb or room and the dangers of
dispossession." Consequently, Hayman remained on familiar
ground as he talked of intruders, almost animalistic struggles
for territory and women, and the violence which "occurs
because animality is unleashed." Likewise, Lois G. Gordon,
in her book on Pinter, merely reaffirmed in all of the plays
a similar pattern: "Within a womblike room rather ordinary
people pursue their rather ordinary business; a mysterious
figure enters, and the commonplace room becomes the vio-
lent scene of their mental and physical breakdown." Ac-
companying this pattern was "light-dark, dry-damp, warm-

cold imagery," and these completed the "Pinter mode." Even
John Russell Taylor, in his Harold Pinter, recapitulated
earlier ideas. As he surveyed the entire Pinter canon, he
saw an "unswerving logic with which each play follows on
from the one before, taking up, elaborating or modifying
themes and images." Taylor traced the development and
recurrences of "major themes and images": "the Room,
Menace, Communication, the Family, the Woman, Personality, Perception and Memory."

Martin Esslin's recently published book, The Peopled
Wound, must now be considered the most thorough study of
Pinter's work. Recognizing the danger of "easy generalisa-
tions" about the playwright, Esslin commented on each play
individually and attempted, by means of a "psychoanalytical
approach," to explain "the impact and effect on the audiences,
who obviously respond to the subconscious content of much
that would otherwise remain enigmatic and inexplicable."
Despite the depth of his discussion, however, Esslin offered
few original ideas; rather he seemed to draw together many
earlier ideas, even though he did not make any direct evalu-
ation of the criticism. He described the "core" of Pinter's
drama an expression of "man's existential fear, not as an
abstraction, not as a surreal phantasmagoria, but as something real, ordinary, and acceptable as an everyday occur-
rence." The playwright's ambiguities and ambivalences
reflect "a genuine perplexity about the nature of our experience of the world . . . . " Admitting that he could offer
only a "provisional" judgment about Pinter, Esslin expressed
his belief that the writer's plays "will surely endure not only
as works of brilliant craftsmanship . . . but as considerable
artistic achievements."

Academic material from 1968 and 1969 served as a

final example of the processes of the fashion in which
Pinter remains caught. Unlike the reviewers of the recent
production, whose vociferous negativism might indicate the
final abandonment by fashion, scholars continued enthusias-
tically to see Pinter as a literary notable and to weave
elaborate interpretations about his work. Unfortunately,
their interpretations, merely repeating the old ideas with
different words and emphases, also exhibited the stagnation
brought about by fashion.

XII

This essay, which begins as a study of material
written about Harold Pinter, must finally concentrate on the
complex processes of theatrical fashion. Although commentators advanced many perceptive analyses, most of their
voluminous commentary, as Glenn Loney commented in his
review of the Broadway production of The Homecoming,
reflected, not Pinter, but rather the assumptions of the
theatrical environment in which the author writes.
Despite the many warnings, reviewers and scholars
continued to treat the playwright's pieces as abstractions,
categorizing them, analyzing them in ever more subtle ways,
and in many cases loudly condemning them on the bases of
these analyses. Critics used first one term and then, in
rapid succession, others to define the various movements
within which Pinter supposedly belongs. As each term inevitably failed, commentators moved more strongly towards
the conception of the "Pinteresque." Yet there could be
only a pseudo-progress, for, as very recent reviews showed,
"Pinterism," like any other abstraction, must invariably limit

the playwright. As Ronald Hayman noted, such terms became misleading because they suggested "that what's typical of
him at one stage of his development is also typical of every
other, that his style has remained at a standstill." In an
interview, Pinter responded to the mention of "Pinteresque":
"That word! These damn words and that word Pinteresque
particularly--I don't know what they're bloody well talking
about! I think its a great burden for me to carry, and for
other writers to carry . . . . "[5] As his comment indicated,
the stifling pressures of fashion endangered the creative
artist, just as they led critics to sterile criticism.

Another perspective for this volume of writing about
Pinter must come from the reminder that he has been working for only slightly over a decade. It is too soon to decide
that he is more than a good writer. Only confusion can
come from attempts to say otherwise at this point. The
serious issues raised by reviewers for each play, consequently, were in radical opposition to the subtle readings offered
by those commentators who viewed Pinter as a prominent
literary figure. In his Harold Pinter, John Russell Taylor
restated the earlier warning given by Martin Esslin: "It is
easy to make approving (or maybe disapproving) noises about
[Pinter's] work; far harder to place him in any dramatic
hierarchy, in Britain or in the world at large. Debate as
to whether he is a 'major' dramatist, for example, seems
not only premature--who can know until posterity has decided
the matter?--but heavily dependent on the criteria brought to
bear, some of which, central to you, may seem totally irrelevant to me, and vice versa."

Arnold P. Hinchliffe was to some extent correct when
he justified his book about "a dramatist who is . . . only
at the beginning of his career" by asserting that "the business

of criticism is to dive in as soon as possible, especially
when simple plays prove so apparently puzzling." But the
accumulated material on Pinter demonstrates that criticism
can attempt to exhaust creative works before they have had
a chance to be tested by posterity. Just as the fashion
interferes with the response to plays in the theatre, as Wardle pointed out, it also sways the academic world toward
overly subtle and needlessly repetitious readings of the
author's plays. Pinter himself stated on the last subject:
"I think . . . that this is an age of such overblown publi-
city and overemphatic pinning down. I'm a very good example
of a writer who can write, but I'm just a writer; and I think
that I've been overblown tremendously because there's a
dearth of really fine writing, and people tend to make too
much of a meal."[6] His commentators have done much worse
by not listening to him.

Notes

1. For complete bibliographic citation on critical items
    discussed in this essay, the reader should consult
    the accompanying checklist of works about Pinter.
    In each case, sufficient information will be provided
    in context to enable the reader to locate the particu-
    lar item. Only material not included in the checklist
    will be footnoted.

2. e.g., H. Thompson, "Harold Pinter Replies," New
    Theatre Magazine, II (January 1961), 8-10; Harold
    Pinter, "Writing for Myself," Twentieth Century,
    CLXIX (February 1961), 172-175; H. Thompson, "Pinter
    Between the Lines, London Sunday Times, March 4,
    1962, p. 25; and Lawrence M. Bensky, "The Art of
    the Theatre III. Harold Pinter," Paris Review, X
    (Fall 1966), 13-37 [Reprinted in Writers at Work, Third
    Series (New York: Viking Press, 1967), pp. 347-368].

3. e.g., the first two interviews cited in note 2 and
    Maurice Zolotow, "Young Man with a Scorn,"
    New York Times, September 17, 1961, Sec. II, p. 3.
    For a discussion of exerpts of the television inter-
    views, see Martin Esslin's The Theatre of the Absurd.

4. See Martin Esslin, "The Theatre of the Absurd Recon-
    sidered," cited in the checklist. Esslin wrote: "What
    I intended as a generic concept, a working hypothesis
    for the understanding of a large number of extremely
    varied and elusive phenomena, has assumed for many
    people, including some drama critics, a reality as
    concrete and as specific as a branded product of the
    detergent industry." To ask an artist if he agrees
    that he is a member of the Theatre of the Absurd,
    Esslin asserted, is to ask "an absurd question" be-
    cause the artist is not "concerned with anything but his
    vision, his own impulse."

4. Bensky, p. 34.

6. Bensky, p. 35.

Part II

Harold Pinter: A Checklist

The material about Pinter has been divided into four
sections. Section 1 includes only the significant bibliographies
of works about him.   Section 2, Books and Book References,
lists, in addition to first printings of criticism, all of the
book reprints of earlier articles and reviews that have been
located.   In each case reprints have been briefly annotated.
Section 3 includes periodical and newspaper articles that do
not discuss particular play productions; the few book reviews
listed in this section have been indicated.

Reviews of stage and film productions in London and
New York and productions on national radio and television
have been gathered in Section 4.   They are arranged by play
titles, which have been placed in chronological order by dates
of first productions.   Beneath each title, reviews have been
grouped by individual production dates, also in chronological
order.   In those few instances in which a play moved to a
second theatre shortly after its opening, subsequent reviews
have been listed under the first opening date.   To avoid
duplication, reviews of dual productions have been listed only
under the first play in the chronological sequence.   Thus,
for example, there is no separate section for The Room
since it has been produced only with other pieces that occur
prior to it in the sequence (see the listings for A Slight
Ache and The Dumb Waiter).   Lone reviews of minor productions have been arranged in a Miscellaneous category

at the end.

Since <u>Night Out</u>, <u>Night School</u>, <u>Night</u>, and the revue sketches are definitely minor works, reviews of their productions have been omitted. Foreign language items have also been excluded. In the case of the most recent production of <u>Landscape</u> and <u>Silence</u>, the bibliography necessarily remains incomplete. Because Pinter's career is still young, this checklist can be considered only preliminary. Any additions--or corrections--will be welcome.

I wish to express my sincerest thanks to Dr. Jackson R. Bryer, for his valuable guidance in this project and for his comments on an early version of it, and to my wife Michelle, without whose assistance and encouragement it could not have been completed. I am also indebted to the Library of Congress; the University of Maryland Library; the New York Public Library; the University of Michigan Library; and Harvard University Library.

1. BIBLIOGRAPHIES

Adelman, Irving, and Rita Dworkin. "Harold Pinter." In
their Modern Drama. Metuchen, N.J.: Scarecrow Press,
1967, pp. 241-242.

Gordon, Lois G. "Pigeonholing Pinter: A Bibliography,"
Theatre Documentation, I (Fall 1968), 3-20.

2. BOOKS AND BOOK REFERENCES

Blau, Herbert. The Impossible Theatre. A Manifesto. New
York: Macmillan, 1964, pp. 254-256.

Bradbrook, Muriel C. English Dramatic Form: A History
of its Development. New York: Barnes and Noble, 1965,
pp. 188-190.

Brown, John Russell. "Dialogue in Pinter and Others." In
his (ed.) Modern British Dramatists. Englewood Cliffs,
N.J.: Prentice-Hall, 1968, pp. 122-144. [Reprinted from
Critical Quarterly, VII (Autumn 1965), 223-243.]

_____. "Introduction." In his (ed.) Modern British
Dramatists. Englewood Cliffs, N.J.: Prentice-Hall,
1968, pp. 1-14.

_____. "Mr. Pinter's Shakespeare." In Morris Freed-
man, ed. Essays in the Modern Drama. Boston: D. C.
Heath, 1964, pp. 352-366. [Reprinted from Critical
Quarterly, V (Autumn 1963), 251-265.]

Brustein, Robert. "A Naturalism of the Grotesque." In his
Seasons of Discontent. New York: Simon and Schuster,
1965, pp. 180-183. [Reprinted from New Republic, CXLV
(October 23, 1961), 29-30.]

_____. The Theatre of Revolt. Boston: Little, Brown
and Co., 1964, pp. 26-27.

95

_____. "Thoughts from Abroad." In his The Third
Stage. New York: Alfred A. Knopf, 1969, pp. 117-122.
[Reprints "Thoughts from Home and Abroad," New
Republic, CLII (June 26, 1965), 29-30 and "Saturn Eats
His Children," New Republic, CLVI (January 28, 1967),
34-36.]

Chiardi, Joseph. Landmarks of Contemporary Drama.
London: Herbert Jenkins Ltd., 1965, pp. 119-126.

Clurman, Harold. "Harold Pinter." In his The Naked Image.
New York: Macmillan, 1966, pp. 105-114. [Reprints
"Theatre," Nation, CXCIII (October 21, 1961), 276;
"Theatre," Nation, CXCV (December 15, 1962), 429-430;
"Theatre," Nation, CXCVIII (January 27, 1964), 106;
and "Theatre," Nation, CXCIX (December 28, 1964), 522-
524.]

Cohn, Ruby. Currents in Contemporary Drama. Blooming-
ton, Indiana: Indiana University Press, 1969, pp. 15-17,
78-81, 177-181.

Davison, Peter. "Contemporary Drama and Popular Dramatic Forms." In Aspects of Drama and the Theatre.
New South Wales: Sydney University Press, 1965, pp.
143-197.

Esslin, Martin. "Godot and His Children: The Theatre of
Samuel Beckett and Harold Pinter." In William A. Arm-
strong, ed. Experimental Drama. London: G. Bell
and Sons, 1963, pp. 128-146. [Reprinted in John Russell
Brown, ed. Modern British Dramatists. Englewood
Cliffs, N.J.: Prentice-Hall, 1968, pp. 58-70.]

_____. "New Form in the Theatre." In his Reflections:
Essays on Modern Theatre. Garden City, New York:
Doubleday, 1969, pp. 3-10.

_____. The Peopled Wound: The Work of Harold Pinter.
Garden City, New York: Doubleday, 1970.

_____. The Theatre of the Absurd. Garden City, New
York: Doubleday, 1961, pp. 198-217; Garden City, New
York: Doubleday, 1969, pp. 231-257.

_____. "The Theatre of the Absurd Reconsidered." In his
Reflections: Essays on Modern Theatre. Garden City, New
York: Doubleday, 1969, pp. 183-191.

Fraser, George Sutherland. The Modern Writer and His
World, Revised. Baltimore: Penguin Books, 1964, pp.
238-243.

Freedman, Morris. The Moral Impulse. Carbondale and
Edwardsville: Southern Illinois University Press, 1967,
pp. 124-126.

Gascoigne, Bamber. Twentieth-Century Drama. London:
Hutchinson and Co., 1962, pp. 206-207.

Gassner, John. "Foray into the Absurd." In his Dramatic
Soundings. New York: Crown, 1968, pp. 503-507.
[Reprints "Broadway in Review," Educational Theatre
Journal, XIII (December 1961), 294-296.]

_____. "Osborne and Pinter." In his The World of
Contemporary Drama. New York: American Library
Association, 1965, pp. 21-23.

Gordon, Lois G. Stratagems to Uncover Nakedness.
Columbia, Missouri: University of Missouri Press, 1969.

Hayman, Ronald. Harold Pinter. London: Heinemann,
1968; Second ed. London: Heinemann, 1969. [Second
ed. is expanded to include discussions of Landscape,
Silence, and Night.]

Hinchliffe, Arnold P. Harold Pinter. New York: Twayne
Publishers, 1967.

Kerr, Walter. "The Caretaker." In his The Theatre in
Spite of Itself. New York: Simon and Schuster, 1963,
pp. 116-119.

_____. Harold Pinter. New York: Columbia University
Press, 1967.

_____. "The Hey, Wait a Minute Theater." In his
Thirty Plays Hath November. New York: Simon and
Schuster, 1969, pp. 29-41.

_____. "The Moment of Pinter." In his Thirty Plays
Hath November. New York: Simon and Schuster, 1969,
pp. 41-46. [Reprints "Put Off--Or Turned On--By
Pinter?" New York Times, October 15, 1967, Sec. II,
p. 1.]

Kershaw, John. "The Caretaker." In his The Present
Stage. London: Collins, 1966, pp. 70-87.

Kitchin, Laurence. "Compressionism. The Form." In his
Drama in the Sixties. London: Faber and Faber, 1966,
pp. 45-53.

_____. Mid-Century Drama, Second ed. London: Faber
and Faber, 1962, pp. 119-122.

Leech, Clifford. "Two Romantics: Arnold Wesker and Harold Pinter." In John Russell Brown and Bernard Harris,
eds. Contemporary Theatre. London: Edward Arnold,
1962, pp. 11-31.

Lumley, Frederick. "Harold Pinter." In his New Trends
in Twentieth Century Drama. London: Barrie and
Rockliff, 1967, pp. 266-273.

MacNeice, Louis. Varieties of Parable. Cambridge,
England: Cambridge University Press, 1965, pp. 121-123.

Matthews, Honor. The Primal Curse. London: Chatto and
Windus, 1967, pp. 22-23, 198-201.

Milne, Tom. "The Hidden Face of Violence." In Charles
Marowitz, ed. The Encore Reader. London: Methuen,
1965, pp. 115-124. [Reprinted from Encore, VII
(January-February 1960), 14-20.]

_____. "The Hidden Face of Violence." In John Russell
Brown, ed. Modern British Dramatists. Englewood
Cliffs, N.J.: Prentice-Hall, 1968, pp. 38-46. [Reprinted
from Encore, VII (January-February 1960), 14-20.]

Muir, Kenneth. "Verse and Prose." In John Russell Brown
and Bernard Harris, eds. Contemporary Theatre.
London: Edward Arnold, 1962, pp. 97-115.

Nelson, Hugh. "The Homecoming: Kith and Kin." In John
Russell Brown, ed. Modern British Dramatists. Englewood Cliffs, N.J.: Prentice-Hall, 1968, pp. 145-163.

Nicoll, Allardyce. English Drama: A Modern Viewpoint.
New York: Barnes and Noble, 1968, pp. 140-144.

Prideaux, Tom. "The Adventurous Play--Stranger to

Broadway." In Thomas E. Sanders, ed. The Discovery of Drama. Glenview, Ill.: Scott, Foresman, 1968, pp. 624-627. [Reprinted from Life, LXII (March 3, 1967), 6.]

Sainer, Arthur. "A Slight Ache." In his The Sleepwalker and the Assassin. New York: Bridgehead Books, 1964, pp. 99-102.

Smallwood, Clyde G. "Harold Pinter." In his Elements of the Existentialist Philosophy in the Theatre of the Absurd. Dubuque, Iowa: Wm. C. Brown, 1966, pp. 140-145.

Smith, R. D. "Back to the Text." In John Russell Brown and Bernard Harris, eds. Contemporary Theatre. London: Edward Arnold, 1962, pp. 117-137.

Styan, J. L. The Dark Comedy. Cambridge, England: Cambridge University Press, 1962, pp. 235-238; "After 'Godot': Ionesco, Genet and Pinter." In his The Dark Comedy, Second Ed. Cambridge, England: Cambridge University Press, 1968, pp. 234-250.

_____. "Television Drama." In John Russell Brown and Bernard Harris, eds. Contemporary Theatre. London: Edward Arnold, 1962, pp. 185-204.

Taylor, John Russell. Harold Pinter. London: Longmans, Green, 1969.

_____. The Rise and Fall of the Well-Made Play. New York: Hill and Wang, 1967, pp. 162-164.

_____. "A Room and Some Views. Harold Pinter." In his The Angry Theatre. New York: Hill and Wang, 1962, pp. 231-261.

Wardle, Irving. "Comedy of Menace." In Charles Marowitz, ed. The Encore Reader. London: Methuen, 1965, pp. 86-91. [Reprinted from Encore, V (September-October 1958), 28-33.]

_____. "There's Music in That Room." In Charles Marowitz, ed. The Encore Reader. London: Methuen, 1965, pp. 129-132. [Reprinted from Encore, VII (July-August 1960), 32-34.]

Wellwarth, George E. "Harold Pinter. The Comedy of

Allusiveness." In his The Theatre of Protest and Paradox. New York: New York University Press, 1964, pp.
197-211.

Williams, Raymond. "The Birthday Party: Harold Pinter."
In his Drama From Ibsen to Brecht. London: Chatto
and Windus, 1968, pp. 322-325.

3. ARTICLES

Amend, Victor E. "Harold Pinter--Some Credits and Some
Debits," Modern Drama, X (September 1967), 165-174.

Arden, John. "The Caretaker," New Theatre Magazine,
No. 4, (July 1960), 29-30.

Ashworth, Arthur. "New Theatre: Ionesco, Beckett,
Pinter," Southerly, XXII (No. 3, 1962), 145-154.

Bernhard, F. J. "Beyond Realism: the Plays of Harold
Pinter," Modern Drama, VIII (September 1965), 185-191.

Blau, Herbert. "Politics and the Theatre," Wascana
Review, II (No. 2, 1967), 5-25.

Bleich, David. "Emotional Origins of Literary Meaning,"
College English, XXXI (October 1969), 30-40.

Boulton, James T. "Harold Pinter: The Caretaker and Other
Plays," Modern Drama, VI (September 1963), 131-140.

Bovie, Palmer. "Seduction: The Amphitryon Theme from
Plautus to Pinter," Minnesota Review, VII (No. 3-4,
1967), 304-313.

Bowen, John. "Accepting the Illusion," Twentieth Century,
CLXIX (February 1961), 153-165.

Brine, Adrian. "MacDavies is no Clochard," Drama, No. 61,
(Summer 1961), 35-37.

Brown, John Russell. "Dialogue in Pinter and Others,"
Critical Quarterly, VII (Autumn 1965), 225-243.

_____. "Mr. Pinter's Shakespeare," Critical Quarterly,
V (Autumn 1963), 251-265.

Brustein, Robert. "The English Stage," Tulane Drama
Review, X (Spring 1966), 127-133.

Bryden, Ronald. "Three Men in a Room," New Statesman,
LXVII (June 26, 1964), 1004.

Burkman, Katherine H. "The Dramatic World of Harold
Pinter: Its Basis in Ritual," Dissertation Abstracts,
XXX (July 1969), 434-A.

_____. "Pinter's A Slight Ache as Ritual," Modern
Drama, XI (December 1968), 326-335.

Canaday, Nicholas, Jr. "Harold Pinter's 'Tea Party': Seeing and Not-Seeing," Studies in Short Fiction, VI (Fall
1969), 580-585. [Discusses short story version.]

"The Caretaker," Punch, CCXXXIX (August 3, 1960), 177.
[Book review.]

Case, L. L. " 'The Ticket' Or Pinter Parodied," New York
Times, May 16, 1965, Sec. II, p. 6.

Cohen, Mark. "The Plays of Harold Pinter," Jewish
Quarterly, VIII (Summer 1961), 21-22.

Cohn, Ruby. "The Absurdly Absurd: Avatars of Godot,"
Comparative Literature Studies, II (1965), 233-240.

_____. "Latter Day Pinter," Drama Survey, III (Febru-
ary 1964), 367-377.

_____. "The World of Harold Pinter," Tulane Drama
Review, VI (March 1962), 55-68.

Conlon, Patrick O. "Social Commentary in Contemporary
Great Britain, as Reflected in the Plays of John Osborne,
Harold Pinter, and Arnold Wesker," Dissertation Ab-
stracts, XXIX (April 1969), 3713A-3714A.

Cook, David, and Harold F. Brooks. "A Room with Three
Views: Harold Pinter's The Caretaker," Komos, I (June
1967), 62-69.

Craig, H. A. L. "Poetry in the Theatre," New Statesman,
LX (November 12, 1960), 734, 736.

Curley, Daniel. "A Night in the Fun House," Midwest
    Monographs (Univ. of Ill.), Ser. 1, No. 1, (September
    1967), 1-2.

Dias, Earl J. "The Enigmatic World of Harold Pinter,"
    Drama Critique, XI (Fall 1968), 119-124.

Dick, Kay. "Mr. Pinter and the Fearful Matter," Texas
    Quarterly, IV (Autumn 1961), 257-265.

Dillon, Percy C. "The Characteristics of the French
    Theatre of the Absurd in the Plays of Edward Albee and
    Harold Pinter," Dissertation Abstracts, XXIX (July 1968),
    257A-258A.

Douglas, Reid. "The Failure of English Realism," Tulane
    Drama Review, VII (Winter 1962), 180-183.

Dukore, Bernard. "The Theatre of Harold Pinter," Tulane
    Drama Review, VI (March 1962), 43-54.

_____. "A Woman's Place," Quarterly Journal of
    Speech, LII (October 1966), 237-241.

English, Alan C. "A Descriptive Analysis of Harold
    Pinter's Use of Comic Elements in His Stage Plays,"
    Dissertation Abstracts, XXX (April 1970), 4597A-4598A.

Esslin, Martin. "Pinter and the Absurd," Twentieth
    Century, CLXIX (February 1961), 176-185.

_____. "Pinter Translated. On International Non-Com-
    munication," Encounter, XXX (March 1968), 45-47.

Evans, Gareth Lloyd. "Pinter's Black Magic," Manchester
    Guardian, September 30, 1965, p. 8.

Feynman, Alberta E. "The Fetal Quality of 'Character' in
    Plays of the Absurd," Modern Drama, IX (May 1966),
    18-25.

Fletcher, John. "Confrontations: I. Harold Pinter, Roland
    Dubillard, and Eugene Ionesco," Caliban, IV (No. 2, 1967),
    149-152.

Franzblau, Abraham N. "A Psychiatrist Looks at 'The
    Homecoming,'" Saturday Review, L (April 8, 1967), 58.

Free, William J. "Treatment of Character in Harold Pinter's The Homecoming," South Atlantic Bulletin, XXXIV (November 1969), 1-5.

Frisch, Jack E. "Ironic Theatre: Techniques of Irony in the Plays of Samuel Beckett, Eugene Ionesco, Harold Pinter, and Jean Genet," Dissertation Abstracts, XXV (April 1965), 6114-6115.

Gallagher, Kent G. "Harold Pinter's Dramaturgy," Quarterly Journal of Speech, LII (October 1966), 242-248.

Ganz, Arthur. "A Clue to the Pinter Puzzle: The Triple Self in The Homecoming," Educational Theatre Journal, XXI (May 1969), 180-187.

Giannetti, Louis D. "The Drama of the Welfare State," Dissertation Abstracts, XXVIII (July 1967), 229A-230A.

Gilman, Richard. "The Pinter Puzzle," New York Times, January 22, 1967, Sec. II, p. 1.

Goodman, Florence J. "Pinter's The Caretaker: The Lower Depths Descended," Midwest Quarterly, V (January 1964), 117-126.

Hall, John. "British Drama in the Sixties--A Note from London," Texas Quarterly, X (Summer 1967), 15-19.

Hall, Rodney. "Theatre in London," Westerly, No. 3, (October 1964), 57-60.

Hare, Carl. "Creativity and Commitment in the Contemporary British Theatre," Humanities Association Bulletin, XVI (Spring 1965), 21-28.

Hays, H.R. "Transcending Naturalism," Modern Drama, V (May 1962), 27-36.

Hinchliffe, Arnold P. "Mr. Pinter's Belinda," Modern Drama, XI (September 1968), 173-179.

Hoefer, Jacqueline. "Pinter and Whiting: Two Attitudes Towards the Alienated Artist," Modern Drama, IV (February 1962), 402-408.

Hutchings, Patrick. "The Humanism of a Dumb Waiter,"

Westerly, No. 1, (April 1963), 56-63.

Kerr, Walter. "The Theater is the Victim of a Plot,"
New York Times, June 25, 1967, Sec. VI, p. 10.

Kleinman, Neil. "Naming of Names," *Midwest Monographs*
(Univ. of Ill.), Ser. 1, No. 1, (September 1967), 4-5.

Knight, G. Wilson. "The Kitchen Sink," *Encounter,* XXI
(December 1963), 48-54.

Kunkel, Francis L. "The Dystopia of Harold Pinter,"
Renascence, XXI (Autumn 1968), 17-20.

Lahr, John. "The Language of Silence," *Evergreen Review,*
XIII (March 1969), 53-55, 82-90.

_____. "Pinter and Chekhov: the Bond of Naturalism,"
Drama Review, XIII (Winter 1968), 137-145.

_____. "Pinter the Spaceman," *Evergreen Review,* XII
(June 1968), 49-52, 87-90.

Lewis, Peter. "Fascinated by Unsatisfactory People," *Time
and Tide,* XLIII (June 21, 1962), 16-17.

Leyburn, Ellen D. "Comedy and Tragedy Transposed,"
Yale Review, LIII (Summer 1964), 553-562.

Malpas, Edward. "A Critical Analysis of the Stage Plays
of Harold Pinter," *Dissertation Abstracts,* XXVII
(December 1966), 1955A.

Manvell, Roger. "Pinter through French Eyes," *Humanist,*
LXXXIV (May 1969), 142-144.

Marowitz, Charles. "New Wave in a Dead Sea," *X, A
Quarterly Review,* I (October 1960), 270-277.

_____. "'Pinterism' is Maximum Tension through
Minimum Information," *New York Times,* October 1,
1967, Sec. VI, pp. 36-37, 89-90, 92, 94-96.

Mast, Gerald. "Pinter's *Homecoming,*" *Drama Survey,* VI
(Spring 1968), 266-277.

Milne, Tom. "The Hidden Face of Violence," *Encore,* VII

(January-February 1960), 14-20.

Morris, Kelly. "The Homecoming," Tulane Drama Review, XI (Winter 1966), 185-191.

Nelson, Gerald. "Harold Pinter Goes to the Movies," Chicago Review, XIX (No. 1, 1966), 33-43.

Orley, Ray. "Pinter and Menace," Drama Critique, XI (Fall 1968), 124-148.

Parker, R.B. "The Theory and Theatre of the Absurd," Queen's Quarterly, LXXIII (Autumn 1966), 421-441.

Pesta, John. "Pinter's Usurpers," Drama Survey, VI (Spring-Summer 1967), 54-65.

"Pinter Pointers," Times Literary Supplement, July 1, 1965, p. 522. [Book review of The Homecoming.]

Prickett, Stephen. "Three Modern English Plays," Philologica Pragensia, X (No. 1, 1967), 12-21.

"The Reaction Against Realism," Times Literary Supplement, June 30, 1961, p. 400.

Robertson, Roderick. "A Theatre of the Absurd: The Passionate Equation," Drama Survey, II (June 1962), 24-43.

Schechner, Richard. "Puzzling Pinter," Tulane Drama Review, XI (Winter 1966), 176-184.

"Shorter Reviews. The Homecoming," Contemporary Review, CCVIII (February 1966), 112. [Book review.

Sprague, Claire. "Possible or Necessary?" New Theatre Magazine, VIII (No. 1, 1968), 36-37.

States, Bert O. "The Case for Plot in Modern Drama," Hudson Review, XX (Spring 1967), 49-61.

_____. "Pinter's Homecoming: the Shock of Nonrecognition," Hudson Review, XXI (Autumn 1968), 474-486.

Storch, R.F. "Harold Pinter's Happy Families," Massachusetts Review, VIII (Autumn 1967), 703-712.

Sykes, Alrene. "Harold Pinter's Dwarfs, " Komos, I (June
    1967), 70-75.

Taubman, Howard. "Shared Quicksand, " New York Times,
    December 9, 1962, Sec. II, p. 5.

Taylor, John Russell. "British Drama of the Fifties, "
    World Theatre, XI (Autumn 1962), 241-254.

Thompson, Marjorie. "The Image of Youth in the Con-
    temporary Theater, " Modern Drama, VII (February
    1965), 443-445.

Thornton, Peter C. "Blindness and the Confrontation with
    Death: Three Plays by Harold Pinter, " Die Neueren
    Sprachen, n. s. XVII (May 1968), 213-223.

Trilling, Ossia. "The New English Realism, " Tulane
    Drama Review, VII (Winter 1962), 184-193.

Walker, Augusta. "Messages from Pinter, " Modern Drama,
    X (May 1967), 1-10.

Wardle, Irving. "Comedy of Menace, " Encore, V
    (September-October 1958), 28-33.

_____ . "New Waves on the British Stage, " Twentieth
    Century, CLXXII (Summer 1963), 57-65.

Wasson, Richard. "Mime and Dream, " Midwest Monographs
    (Univ. of Ill.), Ser. 1, No. 1, (September 1967), 7-8.

Whiting, John. "Book Reviews, " London Magazine, VII
    (November 1960), 93-94. [The Caretaker and The Birth-
    day Party and Other Plays.]

Winegarten, Renee. "The Anglo-Jewish Dramatist in Search
    of His Soul, " Midstream, XII (October 1966), 40-52.

Wortis, Irving. "The Homecoming, " Library Journal, XCII
    (April 1, 1967), 1508. [Book review.]

Wright, Ian. "Shooting The Caretaker, " Manchester
    Guardian, February 20, 1963, p. 7.

4. PRODUCTION REVIEWS

The Birthday Party

May 19, 1958: Lyric Theatre, Hammersmith

Barber, John. "A Warning Perhaps, But a Bore!" London
Daily Express, May 20, 1958, p. 12.

Boothroyd, J.B. "At the Play," Punch, CCXXXIV (May 28,
1958), 721.

Brien, Alan. "Communications," Spectator, CC (May 30,
1958), 687.

Darlington, W.A. "Mad Meg and Lodger. Play Revels in
Obscurity," London Daily Telegraph, May 20, 1958, p.
10.

Dent, Alan. "Mr. Pinter Misses his Target," London News
Chronicle, May 20, 1958, p. 5.

Granger, Derek. "The Birthday Party," London Financial
Times, May 20, 1958, p. 15.

Hobson, Harold. "Life Outside London," London Sunday
Times, June 15, 1958, p. 11.

_____. "The Screw Turns Again," London Sunday Times,
May 25, 1958, p. 11.

Jackson, Frank. "The New Shows," London Sunday Citizen,
May 25, 1958, p. 7.

M.W.W. "The Birthday Party," Manchester Guardian, May
21, 1958, p. 5.

Myson, Myke. "Horror 'comic,'" London Daily Worker,
May 26, 1958, p. 2.

"Puzzling Surrealism of the Birthday Party," London Times,
May 20, 1958, p. 3.

Shulman, Milton. "Sorry, Mr. Pinter, You're Just Not
Funny Enough," London Evening Standard, May 20, 1958,
p. 6.

Trewin, J.C. "The World of the Theatre. After the Party," Illustrated London News, CCXXXII (May 31, 1958), 932.

Tynan, Kenneth. "At the Theatre. Eastern Approaches," London Observer, May 25, 1958, p. 15.

Wardle, Irving. "The Birthday Party," Encore, V (July-August 1958), 39-40.

Wilson, Cecil. "Cheers for the Mad Guests," London Daily Mail, May 20, 1958, p. 3.

Worsley, T.C. "A New Dramatist, or Two," New Statesman, LV (May 31, 1958), 692, 694.

December 1959: Ealing, England

Alvarez, A. "Death in the Morning," New Statesman, LVIII (December 12, 1959), 836.

March 22, 1960: Independent Television, London

Cooke, Fred. "Mystery," London Reynold News, March 27, 1960, p. 11.

Coton, A.V. "What was the Matter with Stanley?" London Daily Telegraph, March 23, 1960, p. 14.

Crozier, Mary. "Television," Manchester Guardian, March 23, 1960, p. 7.

Diack, Phil. "A Stage Flop is Big Hit," London Daily Herald, March 23, 1960, p. 5.

Hare, Norman. "Miss Withers saves the Show," London News Chronicle, March 22, 1960, p. 5.

Lane, Stewart. "An Eerie Affair," London Daily Worker, March 24, 1960, p. 2.

Purser, Philip. "Mr. Bell's Fare Sums up a Revolution," London News Chronicle, April 25, 1960, p. 3.

Richardson, Maurice. "Oedipus of the Sixth Form," London
Observer, March 27, 1960, p. 25.

Sear, Richard. "A Play to Scorch Nerve Ends," London
Daily Mirror, March 23, 1960, p. 18.

"A Simple Play. The Birthday Party on Television,"
London Times, March 23, 1960, p. 16.

Wiggin, Maurice. "Smaller but Sweeter," London Sunday
Times, March 27, 1960, p. 23.

                June 18, 1964: Aldwych Theatre, London

Brien, Alan. "Pinter's first Play," London Sunday Telegraph, June 21, 1964, p. 10.

Darlington, W. A. "Enjoyable Pinter," London Daily Telegraph, June 19, 1964, p. 18.

Davenport, John. "Plays. Pinter and Brecht," Queen,
CDXXII (July 1, 1964), 8.

Gascoigne, Bamber. "Pinter Makes It all too Plain,"
London Observer, June 21, 1964, p. 24.

Gross, John. "Amazing Reductions," Encounter, XXIII
(September 1964), 50-51.

Hope-Wallace, Philip. "The Birthday Party," Manchester
Guardian, June 19, 1964, p. 11.

Kingston, Jeremy. "At the Play," Punch, CCXLVI (June
24, 1964), 941.

Kretzmer, Herbert. "The Laughs Grow--But Should Pinter
be Happy?" London Daily Express, June 19, 1964, p. 6.

Lambert, J. W. "Trial by Laughter," London Sunday Times,
June 21, 1964, p. 33.

Pacey, Ann. "Pinter's Party Piece," London Daily Herald,
June 19, 1964, p. 5.

"A Slicker and Less Dangerous Pinter," London Times,
June 19, 1964, p. 18.

Sutherland, Jack. "Brilliant, Despairing Pinter," London
    Daily Worker, June 20, 1964, p. 3.

Taylor, John Russell. "Rags to Riches," Plays and
    Players, XI (August 1964), 28-29.

Thirkell, Arthur. "First Night," London Daily Mirror,
    June 19, 1964, p. 18.

Trewin, J.C. "The World of the Theatre. Guessing
    Game," Illustrated London News, CCXLV (July 4, 1964),
    28.

Young, B.A. "The Birthday Party," London Financial
    Times, June 20, 1964, p. 9.

            October 3, 1967: Booth Theatre, New York

Barnes, Clive. "The Theater: Pinter's 'Birthday Party,'"
    New York Times, October 4, 1967, p. 40.

Bermel, Albert. "The Father as Fate," New Leader, L
    (October 23, 1967), 27-28.

Bolton, Whitney. "Harold Pinter's 'The Birthday Party,'"
    New York Morning Telegraph, October 5, 1967, p. 3.

Cavanaugh, Arthur. "Stage," Sign, XLVII (December 1967),
    46.

Chapman, John. "'The Birthday Party' A Whatsit by
    Pinter," New York Daily News, October 4, 1967, p. 86.

Clurman, Harold. "Theatre," Nation, CCV (October 23,
    1967), 412-414.

Cooke, Richard P. "Pinter Party," Wall Street Journal,
    October 5, 1967, p. 16.

Downer, Alan S. "Old, New, Borrowed, and (a Trifle)
    Blue: Notes on the New York Theatre 1967-68,"
    Quarterly Journal of Speech, LIV (October 1968), 199-211.

Gilman, Richard. "Pre-Vintage Pinter," New Republic,
    CLVII (October 21, 1967), 36-38.

Gottfried, Martin. "'The Birthday Party,'" Women's Wear
Daily, CXV (October 4, 1967), 44.

Hewes, Henry. "Disobedience, Civil and Uncivil,"
Saturday Review, L (October 28, 1967), 46-47.

_____. "Like Birth Warmed Over," Saturday Review, L
(October 21, 1967), 50.

Hipp, Edward Sothern. "'The Birthday Party,'" Newark
Evening News, October 4, 1967, p. 66.

Hobe. "The Birthday Party," Variety, CXLVIII (October 11,
1967), 104.

Hughes, Catharine. "'The Birthday Party,' how can I be
certain of what I see?" America, CXVIII (January 6,
1968), 10-12.

Kerr, Walter. "Put Off--Or Turned On--By Pinter?"
New York Times, October 15, 1967, Sec. II, p. 1.

Kroll, Jack. "Blood from Stones," Newsweek, LXX
(October 16, 1967), 104, 106.

Lewis, Theophilus. "The Birthday Party," America,
CXVII (October 28, 1967), 487.

Loney, Glenn. "Broadway in Review," Educational Theatre
Journal, XIX (December 1967), 511-517.

McCarten, John. "Down, way down by the Seaside," New
Yorker, XLIII (October 14, 1967), 151.

"New Plays. The Word as Weapon," Time, XC (October
13, 1967), 71-72.

Simon, John. "Pinter, Boy Soprano," Commonweal,
LXXXVII (October 27, 1967), 122-123.

Streiker, Lowell D. "Pinter: Artificer of Menacing Meaninglessness," Christian Century, LXXXIV (December 13,
1967), 1604.

Watts, Richard, Jr. "An Adventure in Early Pinter,"
New York Post, October 5, 1967, p. 55.

West, Anthony. "The Birthday Party, 'theatre at its very best,'" Vogue, CL (November 1, 1967), 134.

December 9, 1968: Coronet Theater, New York
(Movie version)

Bahrenburg, Bruce. "Birthday Party," Newark Evening News, December 10, 1968, p. 58.

Canby, Vincent. "Screen: Unsettling World of 'The Birthday Party,'" New York Times, December 10, 1968, p. 54.

Guarino, Ann. "Few Happy Returns in Enigmatic 'Party,'" New York Daily News, December 10, 1968, p. 81.

Japa. "The Birthday Party," Variety, CCLIII (December 18, 1968), 26.

Mishkin, Leo. "Birthday Party," New York Morning Telegraph, December 10, 1968, p. 3.

A Slight Ache

July 29, 1959: BBC Third Programme, London (Radio)

"Commonplace into Fantasy," London Times, July 30, 1959, p. 8.

Ferris, Paul. "Radio Notes," London Observer, August 2, 1959, p. 12.

Robinson, Robert. "With Proper Humility," London Sunday Times, August 2, 1959, p. 14.

January 18, 1961: Arts Theatre, London

Cain, Alex Matheson. "Worlds of Fantasy," Tablet, CCXV (February 25, 1961), 178.

Craig, H. A. L. "The Sound of the Words," New Statesman, LXI (January 27, 1961), 152-153.

Darlington, W. A.   "Pinter's Play's Obscurity,"   London
    Daily Telegraph, January 19, 1961, p. 14.

"Entertaining Triple Bill," London Times,   January 19,
    1961, p. 16.

Gascoigne, Bamber.   "Pulling the Wool?"   Spectator, CCVI
    (January 27, 1961),   106.

Hobson, Harold.   "The Arts in Form Again,"   London
    Sunday Times, January 22, 1961, p. 33.

Hope-Wallace, Philip.   "Treble Chance,"   Manchester
    Guardian, January 19, 1961, p. 9.

Keown, Eric.   "At the Play,"   Punch, CCXL (January 25,
    1961), 186.

Levin, Bernard.   "One Times Three is a Sum that Pleases
    Me!" London Daily Express, January 19, 1961, p. 8.

M. M. "Theatre Three," London Daily Worker, January
    20, 1961, p. 3.

Muller, Robert.   "Hate Yourself Though You May, You'll
    Enjoy These Plays," London Daily Mail, January 19,
    1961, p. 3.

Shulman, Milton.   "Three for One Give Mr. Williams an
    Actor's Field Day," London Evening Standard, January
    19, 1961, p. 14.

Trewin, J. C.   "Cutting it Short,"   Illustrated London News,
    CCXXXVIII (February 4, 1961), 192.

Tynan, Kenneth.   "Let Coward Flinch,"   London Observer,
    January 22, 1961, p. 30.

December 9, 1964: Writer's Stage Theater,
New York (With The Room)

Bolton, Whitney. "Pinter Plays Heady, But Foggy, too,"
New York Morning Telegraph, December 11, 1964, p. 2.

Clurman, Harold. "Theatre," Nation, CXCIX (December 28,
1964), 522-524.

Cooke, Richard P. "Pinter's Mysteries," Wall Street Journal,
December 11, 1964, p. 16.

Davis, James. "A Good Pinter Drama," New York Daily
News, December 10, 1964, p. 92.

"Finger Exercise in Dread," Time, LXXXIV (December 18,
1964), 86.

Gottfried, Martin. "'The Room'--'A Slight Ache,'" Women's
Wear Daily, CIX (December 10, 1964), 48.

Hewes, Henry. "Matched Pairs," Saturday Review, XLVII
(December 26, 1964), 33.

Kenn. "The New Pinter Plays," Variety, CCXXXVII
(December 16, 1964), 66.

Kerr, Walter. "Kerr Reviews Pinter's 'Room' and 'Slight
Ache,'" New York Herald Tribune, December 10, 1964,
p. 16.

McClain, John. "Pinter Fuzzy in Dual Bill," New York
Journal American, December 10, 1964, p. 19.

"Malice Domestic," Newsweek, LXIV (December 21, 1964),
75-76.

Morris, Ivan. "The Room and A Slight Ache, 'bitter, off-
beat humour,'" Vogue, CXLV (February 1, 1965), 98.

Nadel, Norman. "Pinter is Peerless as Ruler of Enigma,"
New York World Telegram and Sun, December 10, 1964,
p. 13.

Oliver, Edith. "Hooray!" New Yorker, XL (December 19, 1964), 66-71.

Sheed, Wilfrid. "Absurdity Revisited," Commonweal, LXXXII (April 30, 1965), 193-194.

Taubman, Howard. "The Theater: Two Early Pinter Dramas," New York Times, December 10, 1964, p. 62.

Unger, Michael D. "Pinter Plays," Newark Evening News, December 10, 1964, p. 58.

Watts, Richard, Jr. "Two Remarkable Plays by Pinter," New York Post, December 10, 1964, p. 46.

The Dumb Waiter

January 21, 1960: Hampstead Theatre Club,
London (With The Room)

Alvarez, A. "The Arts and Entertainment. Wanted--a Language," New Statesman, LIX (January 30, 1960), 149-150.

Barnes, Clive. "A Mystery that Asks All the Questions," London Daily Express, March 9, 1960, p. 17.

Brien, Alan. "The Guilty Man," Spectator, CCIV (January 29, 1960), 137-138.

Dent, Alan. "He gets his Effect by Silence," London News Chronicle, March 9, 1960, p. 5.

Findlater, Richard. "The Room: The Dumb Waiter," London Financial Times, January 22, 1960, p. 17.

"First Play by Mr. Pinter. The Room Excusably Derivative," London Times, March 9, 1960, p. 4.

Gibbs, Patrick. "People Shut in Private Worlds. Symbolic Plays," London Daily Telegraph, March 9, 1960, p. 14.

Hobson, Harold. "The Dumb Waiter. The Room," London

Sunday Times, March 13, 1960, p. 25.

_____. "Theatre," London Sunday Times, January 24, 1960, p. 23.

_____. "Vagaries of the West End," London Sunday Times, January 31, 1960, p. 23.

Hope-Wallace, Philip. "The Dumb Waiter. The Room," Manchester Guardian, March 9, 1960, p. 7.

Mortlock, C.B. "She's a Poppet," London City Press, March 18, 1960, p. 8.

Nathan, David. "Oh, Mr. Pinter, What a Way to Write a Play," London Daily Herald, March 9, 1960, p. 3.

Pryce-Jones, Alan. "At the Theatre. O'Neill's Last Phase," London Observer, January 24, 1960, p. 21.

Roberts, Peter. "The Dumb Waiter. The Room," Plays and Players, VII (April 1960), 16.

"Strange and Subtle Double Bill," London Times, January 22, 1960, p. 6.

Trewin, J.C. "The World of the Theatre. Thick and Clear," Illustrated London News, CCXXXVI (February 6, 1960), 226.

W.W. "Two Bafflers," London Daily Worker, March 10, 1960, p. 2.

Worsley, T.C. "The Room: The Dumb Waiter," London Financial Times, March 9, 1960, p. 17.

August 10, 1961: Independent Television, London

Davis, Clifford. "Last Night's TV," London Daily Mirror, August 11, 1961, p. 14.

Diack, Phil. "Oh, the Irony of Pinter!" London Daily Herald, August 11, 1961, p. 5.

Gowers, Michael. "This was Vintage Pinter," London Daily Mail, August 11, 1961, p. 3.

Lane, Stewart. "Televiews," London Daily Worker,
     August 12, 1961, p. 2.

Lockwood, Lyn. "Pinter at his Puzzles Again," London
     Daily Telegraph, August 11, 1961, p. 12.

"Loose Grip on Pinter Play," London Times, August 11,
     1961, p. 11.

Spark, Muriel. "An Experiment in Gluttony," London
     Observer, August 13, 1961, p. 19.

Wiggin, Maurice. "Gilt-Edged in Golden Square," London
     Sunday Times, August 13, 1961, p. 32.

                November 26, 1962: Cherry Lane Theater,
                    New York (With The Collection)

Branigan, Alan. "Impressive. Pinter Plays Puzzle and
     Enchant in Village," Newark Evening News, November
     27, 1962, p. 62.

Clurman, Harold. "Theatre," Nation, CXCV (December 15,
     1962), 429-430.

Cooke, Richard P. "Pinter's Technique," Wall Street
     Journal, November 28, 1962, p. 12.

Dash, Thomas R. "Two Ironic Pinter Plays are Vivid and
     Engrossing," Women's Wear Daily, CV (November 27,
     1962), 28.

Gilman, Richard. "Pinter's Hits--and Misses," Common-
     weal, LXXVII (December 28, 1962), 366-367.

Hewes, Henry. "Winter Pinter," Saturday Review, XLV
     (December 15, 1962), 30.

Kenn. "The Dumbwaiter and The Collection," Variety,
     CCXXIX (December 5, 1962), 58.

Kerr, Walter.   "'The Dumbwaiter' and 'The Collection,'"
     New York Herald Tribune, November 27, 1962, p. 20.

McClain, John. "Two New Plays by Pinter Prove Only Irritat-
     ing," New York Journal American, November 27, 1962, p.
     17.

Nadel, Norman. "Two Pinter Plays at Cherry Lane,"
    New York World Telegram and Sun, November 27, 1962,
    p. 20.

O'Gorman, Ned. "Entertainment," Jubilee, XI (December
    1963), 40.

Oliver, Edith. "Comedies of Terror," New Yorker, XXXVIII
    (December 8, 1962), 148-150.

"Pinter Patter," Time, LXXX (December 7, 1962), 72-73.

Pryce-Jones, Alan. "Openings/New York," Theatre Arts,
    XLVII (January 1963), 10-11.

"Split Level," Newsweek, LX (December 10, 1962), 58.

Taubman, Howard. "Harold Pinter: His 'Dumbwaiter' and
    'Collection' Arrive," New York Times, November 27,
    1962, p. 44.

"Two One-Act Plays by Harold Pinter," New York Morning
    Telegraph, November 28, 1962, p. 2.

Watts, Richard, Jr. "A Pair of Striking Dramas by
    Britain's Harold Pinter," New York Post, November 27,
    1962, p. 62.

The Caretaker

April 27, 1960: Arts Theatre, London

Alvarez, A. "The Arts and Entertainment. Olivier Among
    the Rhinos," New Statesman, LIX (May 7, 1960), 666-667.

Brien, Alan. "Chelsea Beaujolais," Spectator, CCIV (May
    6, 1960), 661-662.

_____. "Something Blue," Spectator, CCIV (June 10,
    1960), 835-836.

"The Caretaker's New Home. Brilliant Production," London
    Times, May 31, 1960, p. 4.

Carthew, Anthony. "This is the Best Play in London,"
London Daily Herald, April 28, 1960, p. 3.

Darlington, W.A. "Actability of Harold Pinter. The
Caretaker," London Daily Telegraph, May 31, 1960, p. 14.

Dennis, Nigel. "Optical Delusions," Encounter, XV (July
1960), 63-66.

Dent, Alan. "Tragedy of a Tramp Alarms Me," London
News Chronicle, May 31, 1960, p. 3.

Donoghue, Denis. "London Letter: Moral West End,"
Hudson Review, XIV (Spring 1961), 93-103.

Gibbs, Patrick. "Mr. Pinter Returns to Enigma," London
Daily Telegraph, April 28, 1960, p. 14.

Gilderdale, Michael. "Spellbinder Made of Three Men,"
London News Chronicle, April 28, 1960, p. 3.

Gilliatt, Penelope. "Comedy of Menace," Queen, CCXVI
(May 25, 1960), 21-22.

Hobson, Harold. "Things are Looking Up," London Sunday
Times, June 5, 1960, p. 25.

Keown, Eric. "At the Play," Punch, CCXXXVIII (May 11,
1960), 665.

Lambert, J.W. "The Caretaker," London Sunday Times,
May 1, 1960, p. 25.

Levin, Bernard. "There's Truth in This Man's Every
Twitch," London Daily Express, May 2, 1960, p. 4.

_____. "Three-Line Cut Lets Everyone See This Play,"
London Daily Express, May 31, 1960, p. 16.

M.M. "A Collection of Characters," London Daily Worker,
April 29, 1960, p. 2.

Mannes, Marya. "Just Looking, Thanks," Reporter, XXIII
(October 13, 1960), 48-51.

Minogue, Valerie. "Taking Care of the Caretaker," Twentieth Century, CLXVIII (September 1960), 243-248.

Mortimer, John. "Now This is What I call Great Acting,"
   London Evening Standard, May 31, 1960, p. 12.

Mortlock, C.B. "Sir Laurence With No Heroics," London
   City Press, May 6, 1960, p. 13.

_____. "Two Casualties," London City Press, June 3,
   1960, p. 10.

Muller, Robert. "The Small World of Harold Pinter,"
   London Daily Mail, April 30, 1960, p. 3.

Panter-Downes, Mollie. "Letter from London," New Yorker,
   XXXVI (July 9, 1960), 57-61.

Pryce-Jones, Alan. "Through the Looking-Glass," London
   Observer, May 1, 1960, p. 23.

Richards, Dick. "Subtle Goonery," London Daily Mirror,
   May 31, 1960, p. 18.

Roberts, Peter. "The Caretaker," Plays and Players, VII
   (July 1960), 15.

Rosselli, John. "Between Farce and Madness," Manchester
   Guardian, April 29, 1960, p. 13.

"A Slight Play that Pleases and Dazes," London Times,
   April 28, 1960, p. 6.

Smith, Lisa Gordon. "The Caretaker," Plays and Players,
   VII (June 1960), 17.

Thompson, J.W.M. "High Voltage Shocks," London Evening
   Standard, April 28, 1960, p. 19.

Trewin, J.C. "The World of the Theatre. Four in Hand,"
   Illustrated London News, CCXXXVI (May 14, 1960), 850.

Tynan, Kenneth. "A Verbal Wizard in the Suburbs," London
   Observer, June 5, 1960, p. 16.

Wardle, Irving. "Revolt Against the West End," Horizon,
   V (January 1963), 26-33.

_____. "There's Music in That Room," Encore, VII (July-
   August 1960), 32-34.

West, Richard. "Extraordinary," London Daily Mirror,
    April 28, 1960, p. 26.

Worsley, T.C. "The Caretaker," London Financial Times,
    April 28, 1960, p. 19.

        October 4, 1961: Lyceum Theater, New York

"Bad Times with a Bum in the House," Life, LI (November
    17, 1961), 195-196.

Black, Susan M. "Play Reviews," Theatre Arts, XLV
    (December 1961), 8-13.

Bolton, Whitney. "'Caretaker' is Vivid, Intensely Satisfying,"
    New York Morning Telegraph, October 6, 1961, p. 2.

Brustein, Robert. "A Naturalism of the Grotesque," New
    Republic, CXLV (October 23, 1961), 29-30.

Chapman, John. "Donald Pleasence Superb Actor and 'Care-
    taker' Splendid Play," New York Daily News, October 5,
    1961, p. 73.

Clurman, Harold. "Theatre," Nation, CXCIII (October 21,
    1961), 276.

Coleman, Robert. "'Caretaker' Cheered; Oh, Well!" New
    York Mirror, October 5, 1961, p. 28.

Cotter, Jerry. "The New Plays," Sign, XLI (December 1961),
    48.

Dash, Thomas R. "Prize Play From London Gets No Gar-
    lands Here," Women's Wear Daily, CIII (October 5, 1961),
    44.

Downer, Alan S. "Experience of Heroes: Notes on the New
    York Theatre, 1961-62," Quarterly Journal of Speech,
    XLVIII (October 1962), 261-270.

Driver, Tom F. "On the Way to Madness," Christian
    Century, LXXVIII (November 22, 1961), 1403-1406.

Dunne, J.G. "Haunting Simple Denial," National Review,
    XI (December 16, 1961), 424.

"Eccentrics in the Attic," Newsweek, LVIII (October 16, 1961), 101.

Gassner, John. "Broadway in Review," Educational Theatre Journal, XIII (December 1961), 294-296.

Gilman, Richard. "Reflections at Midterm," Commonweal, LXXV (December 22, 1961), 339-340.

_____. "Straightforward Mystification," Commonweal, LXXV (October 27, 1961), 122-123.

Hewes, Henry. "Nothing Up the Sleeve," Saturday Review, XLIV (October 21, 1961), 34.

Hipp, Edward Sothern. "'Caretaker' Excels," Newark Evening News, October 5, 1961, p. 54.

Hobe. "The Caretaker," Variety, CCXXXIV (October 11, 1961), 70, 72.

Kerr, Walter. "'The Caretaker,'" New York Herald Tribune, October 5, 1961, p. 16.

Lewis, Robert. "The Quality of Imports," New Leader, XLIV (December 11, 1961), 31.

Lewis, Theophilus. "The Caretaker," America, CVI (December 9, 1961), 376.

McClain, John. "Entrancing, Unusual Drama," New York Journal American, October 5, 1961, p. 19.

Nadel, Norman. "'The Caretaker' at Lyceum," New York World Telegram and Sun, October 5, 1961, p. 16.

Oliver, Edith. "The Bum in the Attic," New Yorker, XXXVII (October 14, 1961), 162-166.

"People are talking about. . . ," Vogue, CXXXIX (January 15, 1962), 38-39.

Roberts, Edwin A., Jr. "A Very Cluttered Room," Wall Street Journal, October 6, 1961, p. 10.

Simon, John. "Theatre Chronicle," Hudson Review, XIV (Winter 1961-1962), 586-592.

Taubman, Howard. "A Leap Foreward: Pinter Makes
    Progress in 'The Caretaker,'" New York Times, October
    15, 1961, Sec. II, p. 1.

_____. "Theatre: Modern Parable of Scorn and Sorrow,"
    New York Times, October 5, 1961, p. 42.

"Unwrapping Mummies," Time, LXXVIII (October 13, 1961),
    58.

Watts, Richard, Jr. "An Absorbing New British Drama,"
    New York Post, October 5, 1961, p. 57.

            January 20, 1964: Guild Theater, New York
                    (Movie, retitled The Guest)

Cook, Alton. "'The Guest' Lacks Stage Version's Force,"
    New York World Telegram and Sun, January 21, 1964,
    p. 12.

Crist, Judith. "Movie Dims Stage's Magic," New York
    Herald Tribune, January 21, 1964, p. 12.

Crowther, Bosley. "Screen: Unruly and Irritating Visitor,"
    New York Times, January 21, 1964, p. 25.

Didion, Joan. "The Guest 'narcoleptic dialogue,'" Vogue,
    CXLIII (March 1, 1964), 57.

Hale, Wanda. "Pleasence Perfect in 'The Guest,'" New
    York Daily News, January 21, 1964, p. 39.

"Life can be Ghastly," Newsweek, LXIII (February 10, 1964),
    84.

Mishkin, Leo. "'The Guest' Weird, Fascinating Film,"
    New York Morning Telegraph, January 21, 1964, p. 2.

Pelswick, Rose. "British Entry Has Vague Story Line,"
    New York Journal American, January 21, 1964, p. 11.

Winsten, Archer. "Reviewing Stand," New York Post,
    January 21, 1964, p. 44.

January 30, 1964: Players Theatre, Greenwich Village

Bolton, Whitney. "'Caretaker' Still Exerts Fascination,"
New York Morning Telegraph, February 1, 1964, p. 2.

Crist, Judith. "'Caretaker'--New House Not Enough,"
New York Herald Tribune, January 31, 1964, p. 8.

Funke, Lewis. "Theater: 'The Caretaker,'" New York
Times, January 31, 1964, p. 16.

Gottfried, Martin. "The Caretaker," Women's Wear Daily,
CVIII (January 31, 1964), 24.

Harris, Leonard. "Grandly Absurd, That's Pinter,"
New York World Telegram and Sun, January 31, 1964, p.
15.

Kenn. "The Caretakers [sic]," Variety, CCXXXIII (February
12, 1964), 82.

Palatsky, Gene. "Dramatic Revival," Newark Evening News,
January 31, 1964, p. 14.

Thompson, Jack. "Perfect Work in 'Caretaker,'" New York
Journal American, January 31, 1964, p. 19.

Watts, Richard, Jr. "Revival of a Remarkable Drama,"
New York Post, January 31, 1964, p. 30.

March 12, 1964: Academy, London (Movie)

Butcher, Maryvonne. "Achtung!" Tablet, CCXVIII (March 14,
1964), 301-302.

Coleman, John. "The Road to Sidcup," New Statesman,
LXVII (March 13, 1964), 423.

Gibbs, Patrick. "'The Caretaker' in Close-up," London
Daily Telegraph, March 13, 1964, p. 13.

Gilliatt, Penelope. "The Conversion of a Tramp," London
Observer, March 15, 1964, p. 24.

Hibbin, Nina. "Wistful, Engaging--But in the end, a Bore,"
    London Daily Worker, March 14, 1964, p. 3.

Oakes, Philip. "Pinter's Worthy Pioneer," London Sunday
    Telegraph, March 15, 1964, p. 14.

Pacey, Ann. "Three Men in a House of Dreams," London
    Daily Herald, March 13, 1964, p. 6.

Powell, Dilys. "Solitaries in an Attic," London Sunday
    Times, March 15, 1964, p. 33.

Richards, Dick. "Talent in the Attic," London Daily Mirror,
    March 13, 1964, p. 21.

October 25, 1966: Associated-Rediffusion Television, London

Banks-Smith, Nancy. "In my View," London Sun, October 26,
    1966, p. 16.

Clayton, Sylvia. "Close-Ups Aid 'Caretaker' Hypnotism,"
    London Daily Telegraph, October 26, 1966, p. 17.

Eastaugh, Kenneth. "A Sorry Version of Pinter's Play,"
    London Daily Mirror, October 26, 1966, p. 18.

Lane, Stewart. "Those Swinging, Way-Out Trendsetters
    Were a Drag," London Morning Star, October 29, 1966,
    p. 2.

"Well's Despairing View of the Future," London Times,
    October 26, 1966, p. 14.

Woodforde, John. "Shock Around the Clock," London Sun-
    day Telegraph, October 30, 1966, p. 11.

The Dwarfs

December 2, 1960: BBC Third Programme, London (Radio)

Ferris, Paul. "Radio Notes," London Observer, December
    11, 1960, p. 26.

"Mr. Pinter at His Most Subtle," London Times, December
   3, 1960, p. 10.

Robinson, Robert. "Radio," London Sunday Times,
   December 25, 1960, p. 32.

             September 18, 1963: Arts Theatre, London
                      (With The Lover)

Bernhard, F. J. "English Theater 1963: In the Wake of the
   New Wave," Books Abroad, XXXVIII (Spring 1964), 143-
   144.

Boothroyd, Basil. "At the Play," Punch, CCXLV (September 25, 1963), 467.

Browne, E. Martin. "A Peep at the English Theatre, Fall
   1963," Drama Survey, III (February 1964), 413-416.

Bryden, Ronald. "Atavism," New Statesman, LXVI
   (September 27, 1963), 420.

Darlington, W. A. "Pinter at his most Pinteresque,"
   London Daily Telegraph, September 19, 1963, p. 16.

Forster, Peter. "Back to the Saltmines," London Sunday
   Telegraph, September 22, 1963, p. 12.

Gascoigne, Bamber. "Love in the Afternoon," London
   Observer, September 22, 1963, p. 26.

Hall, Stuart. "The Lover and The Dwarfs," Encore, X
   (November-December 1963), 47-49.

Hobson, Harold. "The Importance of Fantasy," London
   Sunday Times, September 22, 1963, p. 33.

Hope-Wallace, Philip. "Two Pinter Plays," Manchester
   Guardian, September 19, 1963, p. 9.

J. S. "Pinter and the Malignant Dwarfs," London Daily
   Worker, September 20, 1963, p. 2.

Kretzmer, Herbert. "Freaky Night at the Pintermime,"
   London Daily Express, September 19, 1963, p. 4.

Levin, Bernard. "My Index Finger Itches," London Daily
    Mail, September 20, 1963, p. 3.

Lewis, Jack. "The Little Man's Secret Urge to Kill,"
    London Sunday Citizen, September 22, 1963, p. 22.

Nathan, David. "Pinter's Poetic but Puzzling Private
    World," London Daily Herald, September 19, 1963, p. 3.

Pryce-Jones, David. "Myths in the Living Room,"
    Spectator, CCXI (September 27, 1963), 386.

Shulman, Milton. "The Private, Padded World of Mr.
    Pinter," London Evening Standard, September 19, 1963,
    p. 4.

Taylor, John Russell. "Half Pints of Pinter," Plays and
    Players, XI (November 1963), 38-39.

Thirkell, Arthur. "The Abnormal from Pinter," London
    Daily Mirror, September 19, 1963, p. 18.

Thompson, H. "Mr. Pinter Pursues an Elusive Reality,"
    London Times, September 19, 1963, p. 16.

Worsley, T. C. "The Lover and The Dwarfs," London
    Financial Times, September 20, 1963, p. 26.

_____. "New Pinter Plays, 'Lover' and 'Dwarf,' Of-
    fered in London," New York Times, September 19, 1963,
    p. 21.

January 28, 1968: Public Broadcast Lab, New York (TV)

Bill. "Tele Follow-Up Comment. PBL," Variety, CCXLIX
    (January 31, 1968), 46.

Gould, Jack. "TV: Harold Pinter's Baffling 'Dwarfs,'"
    New York Times, January 29, 1968, p. 63.

Gross, Ben. "Homosexual Play," New York Daily News,
    January 29, 1968, p. 22.

McLaughlin, John. "Harold Pinter and PBL," America,
    CXVIII (February 10, 1968), 193.

The Collection

May 11, 1961: Associated-Rediffusion Television, London

"Ambiguity," Times Literary Supplement, May 12, 1961,
    p. 296.

Black, Peter. "Teleview," London Daily Mail, May 12,
    1961, p. 3.

Diack, Phil. "Here's One Pinter Too Many," London
    Daily Herald, May 12, 1961, p. 4.

"Lightweight but Lively Pinter," London Times, May 12,
    1961, p. 19.

Richardson, Maurice. "Eyes behind the Iron Curtain,"
    London Observer, May 14, 1961, p. 27.

Sear, Richard. "A Glittering Haze," London Daily Mirror,
    May 12, 1961, p. 20.

Shorter, Eric. "Pinter Up in the World. Horrors Round
    the Corner," London Daily Telegraph, May 12, 1961,
    p. 17.

Wiggin, Maurice. "Rag Trade," London Sunday Times,
    May 14, 1961, p. 48.

June 12, 1962: Radio, London

Lewis, Naomi. "Experiments in Listening," London
    Observer, June 17, 1962, p. 24.

Shuttleworth, Martin. "Ambiguities," Listener, LXVII
    (June 21, 1962), 1089-1090.

Wilsher, Peter. "What Happened in Leeds?" London
    Sunday Times, June 17, 1962, p. 44.

June 18, 1962: Aldwych Theatre, London

Brien, Alan. "A World of Wheezes," London Sunday
    Telegraph, June 24, 1962, p. 8.

Cain, Alex Matheson. "Strange Menages," Tablet, CCXVI (June 30, 1962), 624.

Darlington, W.A. "Mr. Pinter's Might-Have-Beens," London Daily Telegraph, June 19, 1962, p. 14.

Foreman, Carl. "Majors and Minors," New Statesman, LXIII (June 22, 1962), 917.

Gascoigne, Bamber. "Cult of Personality," Spectator, CCVIII (June 29, 1962), 857-858.

Higgins, John. "The Collection and Playing with Fire," London Financial Times, June 20, 1962, p. 20.

Hope-Wallace, Philip. "New Pinter Play," Manchester Guardian, June 19, 1962, p. 7.

Keown, Eric. "At the Play," Punch, CCXLII (June 27, 1962), 987.

Kretzmer, Herbert. "The Magic Touch that Falters," London Daily Express, June 19, 1962, p. 4.

Lambert, J.W. "A Stitch in Time," London Sunday Times, June 24, 1962, p. 35.

Lewis, Jack. "The Value of Virtue," London Sunday Citizen, June 24, 1962, p. 8.

Mayersberg, Paul. "Harold Pinter's 'The Collection,'" Listener, LXVIII (July 5, 1962), 26.

Muller, Robert. "An Evening like this Revives One's Faith," London Daily Mail, June 19, 1962, p. 3.

Nathan, David. "Pinter Looks at Loving," London Daily Herald, June 19, 1962, p. 7.

"On the Fence between Farce and Tragedy," London Times, June 19, 1962, p. 13.

Ryan, Stephen P. "The London Stage," America, CVII (October 27, 1962), 956-958.

Shulman, Milton. "Pinter in his Best Hypnotic Mood," London Evening Standard, June 19, 1962, p. 10.

Thirkell, Arthur. "Empty," London Daily Mirror, June 19, 1962, p. 24.

Thompson, H. "A Slight Case of Conversation," London Times, June 23, 1962, p. 4.

Trewin, J.C. "The World of the Theatre. Between the Lines," Illustrated London News, CCXL (June 30, 1962), 1058.

Wardle, Irving. "Laughter in the Wilderness," London Observer, June 24, 1962, p. 23.

The Lover

March 28, 1963: Associated-Rediffusion
Television, London

Bill, Jack. "A Too-Sexy Pinter?" London Daily Mirror, March 28, 1963, p. 18.

"Complex Design of Marriage," London Times, March 29, 1963, p. 15.

Gowers, Michael. "Freud, no doubt, had the Word," London Daily Mail, March 29, 1963, p. 18.

Lane, Stewart. "New Director? Let's Call in the Head Shrinker," London Daily Worker, March 30, 1963, p. 2.

Lockwood, Lyn. "Pinter Play's Message is Received," London Daily Telegraph, March 29, 1963, p. 16.

Potter, Dennis. "Pinter Play a Sizzling Triumph," London Daily Herald, March 29, 1963, p. 7.

Purser, Philip. "Winning a Fixed Race," London Sunday Telegraph, March 31, 1963, p. 13.

Richardson, Maurice. "Pinter Among the Pigeons," London Observer, March 31, 1963, p. 39.

Sear, Richard. "Such an Elegant Love Play," London Daily

Mirror, March 29, 1963, p. 18.

Walsh, Michael. "One Fine Hour with Pinter's Lovers,"
London Daily Express, March 29, 1963, p. 4.

Wiggin, Maurice. "Crime and Punishment," London Sunday
Times, March 31, 1963, p. 39.

January 4, 1964: Cherry Lane Theater, New York

Bolton, Whitney. "Two Off-Beat Plays by Beckett, Pinter,"
New York Morning Telegraph, January 7, 1964, p. 2.

Brustein, Robert. "Mid-Season Gleanings," New Republic,
CL (February 1, 1964), 28, 30.

Clurman, Harold. "Theatre," Nation, CXCVIII (January 27,
1964), 106.

Cooke, Richard P. "Beckett and Pinter," Wall Street
Journal, January 7, 1964, p. 18.

Gilman, Richard. "Patience Rewarded," Commonweal, LXXIX
(January 24, 1964), 484-485.

Gottfried, Martin. "'The Lover' and 'Play,'" Women's
Wear Daily, CVIII (January 6, 1964), 32.

Hewes, Henry. "Intramural Sport," Saturday Review,
XLVII (January 25, 1964), 25.

Kenn. "Play and The Lover," Variety, CCXXXIII (January
22, 1964), 92.

Kerr, Walter. "'Play' and 'The Lover'--Twin Bill at
Cherry Lane," New York Herald Tribune, January 6,
1964, p. 12.

McClain, John. "Two Plays: Abstract But Clear," New
York Journal American, January 6, 1964, p. 13.

Nadel, Norman. "Playgoing is an Adventure with Barr,
Wilder and Albee," New York World Telegram and Sun,
January 6, 1964, p. 14.

Oliver, Edith. "Doing Pinter Proud," New Yorker, XXXIX

(January 11, 1964), 69-70.

Palatsky, Gene. "Cherry Lane Pair Incisive," Newark
    Evening News, January 6, 1964, p. 16.

"Pas de Trois--Twice," Time, LXXXIII (January 17, 1964),
    64.

Popkin, Henry. "The Lover and Play, 'curiosities,'" Vogue,
    CXLIII (February 15, 1964), 22.

Rogoff, Gordon. "Following Beckett," New Leader, XLVII
    (January 20, 1964), 29-30.

Taubman, Howard. "Theater: Dual Offering," New York
    Times, January 6, 1964, p. 35.

Watts, Richard, Jr. "The News of Pinter and Beckett,"
    New York Post, January 6, 1964, p. 16.

The Tea Party

March 25, 1965: BBC Television, London

Black, Peter. "TV," London Daily Mail, March 26, 1965,
    p. 3.

Cooke, Fred. "Pinter," London Sunday Citizen, March 28,
    1965, p. 23.

Davis, Clifford. "Provocative Pinter," London Daily
    Mirror, March 26, 1965, p. 18.

"Disturbing Television Play by Pinter," London Times,
    March 26, 1965, p. 15.

Lane, Stewart. "Pinter's Hero Loses Control of his
    Destiny," London Daily Worker, March 27, 1965, p. 2.

Mitchell, Adrian. "Pinter's Quiet Scream," London Sun,
    March 26, 1965, p. 16.

Purser, Philip. "Sense of Occasion," London Sunday

Telegraph, March 28, 1965, p. 15.

Richardson, Maurice. "Paranoid's Progress," London
Observer, March 28, 1965, p. 25.

Shorter, Eric. "Pinter Hero Who Loses Confidence,"
London Daily Telegraph, March 26, 1965, p. 19.

Wiggin, Maurice. "I'll Let Mine Cool. . . ," London
Sunday Times, March 28, 1965, p. 26.

October 15, 1968: Eastside Playhouse, New York
(With The Basement)

Barnes, Clive. "Theater: The Civilized Violence of Harold
Pinter," New York Times, October 16, 1968, p. 40.

Bolton, Whitney. "Brilliant the Word for Two Pinter
Plays," New York Morning Telegraph, October 23, 1968,
p. 3.

Clurman, Harold. "Theatre," Nation, CCVII (November 4,
1968), 477.

Cooke, Richard P. "A Pair from Pinter," Wall Street
Journal, October 17, 1968, p. 20.

Davis, James. "Two Fine Pinter Plays," New York Daily
News, October 16, 1968, p. 101.

Duberman, Martin. "Theater 69," Partisan Review, XXXVI
(No. 3, 1969), 483-500.

Gottfried, Martin. "New Pinter Plays," Women's Wear
Daily, CXVII (October 16, 1968), 67, 71.

Humm. "Tea Party and The Basement," Variety, CCLII
(October 30, 1968), 75.

Kerr, Walter. "The Something that Pinter Holds Back,"
New York Times, November 3, 1968, Sec. II, p. 7.

Kraft, Daphne. "Two Pinter Plays," Newark Evening News,
October 16, 1968, p. 56.

Kroll, Jack. "Dark Secrets," Newsweek, LXXII (October 28,
1968), 135.

Lewis, Theophilus. "The Teaparty [sic]. The Basement,"
America, CXIX (November 9, 1968), 447.

Oliver, Edith. "Threats and Games," New Yorker, XLIV
(October 26, 1968), 140-141.

Simon, John. "Pinter Is At It Again," New York, I
(November 18, 1968), 44.

"Translations from the Unconscious," Time, XCII (October
25, 1968), 69.

Watts, Richard, Jr. "Two Plays by Harold Pinter," New
York Post, October 16, 1968, p. 87.

Weales, Gerald. "Pinter at Work," Commonweal, LXXXIX
(December 6, 1968), 350-351.

West, Anthony. "Tea Party and The Basement, 'perfect little
machine,' " Vogue, CLII (December 1968), 170.

September 17, 1970: Duchess Theatre, London
(With The Basement)

Barber, John. "Pinter Nightmares of Invaded Privacy,"
London Daily Telegraph, September 19, 1970, p. 9.

Dawson, Helen. "Fledglings in a Limbo," London Observer,
September 20, 1970, p. 25.

Fuller, Peter. "Pinter's Enigmas," London City Press,
September 24, 1970, p. 12.

Hope-Wallace, Philip. "Harold Pinter Double Bill,"
Manchester Guardian, September 18, 1970, p. 8.

Hurren, Kenneth. "Familiar Ground," Spectator, CCXXV
(September 26, 1970), 341-342.

Jones, D.A.N. "Chic and Cute," Listener, LXXXIV
(September 24, 1970), 433.

Lambert, J.W. "Plays in Performance," Drama, No. 99,
(Winter 1970), 22-23.

Marcus, Frank. "End of the Beginning," London Sunday
    Telegraph, September 20, 1970, p. 14.

Nightingale, Benedict. "Outboxed," New Statesman, LXXX
    (September 25, 1970), 394-395.

Shulman, Milton. "Now You See it, Now You Don't. . .,"
    London Evening Standard, September 18, 1970, p. 25.

Taylor, John Russell. "Tea Party and The Basement,"
    Plays and Players, XVIII (November 1970), 36-39.

Wardle, Irving. "Pinter Propriety," London Times,
    September 18, 1970, p. 6.

Wells, John. "Theatre," Punch, CCLIX (September 30,
    1970), 482-483.

Whitemore, Hugh. "Plays," Queen, CDXXXVI (Late
    October 1970), 97.

The Homecoming

            June 3, 1965: Aldwych Theatre, London

Benedictus, David. "Pinter's Errors," Spectator, CCXIV
    (June 11, 1965), 755, 758.

Brien, Alan. "In London: The Homecoming, 'an unnerving
    horror-comic skill, '" Vogue, CXLVI (September 15, 1965),
    75.

Browne, E. Martin. "A First Look Round the English Theatre,
    1965," Drama Survey, IV (Summer 1965), 177.

Brustein, Robert. "Thoughts from Home and Abroad,"
    New Republic, CLII (June 26, 1965), 29-30.

Bryden, Ronald "A Stink of Pinter," New Statesman, LXIX
    (June 11, 1965), 928.

Curtis, Anthony. "Among Men," London Sunday Telegraph,
    June 6, 1965, p. 10.

Gilliatt, Penelope. "Achievement from a Tight-Rope,"
London Observer, June 6, 1965, p. 25.

Hall, Stuart. "Home Sweet Home," Encore, XII (July-
August 1965), 30-34.

Hobson, Harold. "Pinter Minus the Moral," London Sunday
Times, June 6, 1965, p. 39.

Holland, Mary. "Theatre," Queen, CDXXIV (June 16, 1965),
15.

Hope-Wallace, Philip. "Pinter's 'The Homecoming,'"
Manchester Guardian, June 4, 1965, p. 11.

Kingston, Jeremy. "Theatre," Punch, CCXLVIII (June 16,
1965), 901.

Lewis, Jack. "Macabre," London Sunday Citizen, June 6,
1965, p. 25.

Mortlock, C.B. "The Homecoming," London City Press,
June 25, 1965, p. 11.

Nathan, David. "Same Again from Puzzling Mr. Pinter,"
London Sun, June 4, 1965, p. 10.

O'Connor, Patrick. "Theatre," Furrow, XVI (August 1965),
495-497.

Panter-Downes, Mollie. "Letter from London," New Yorker,
XLI (July 31, 1965), 59-66.

Shorter, Eric. "Outrageous and Gruesomely Funny Play,"
London Daily Telegraph, June 4, 1965, p. 18.

Smith, Warren S. "The New Plays in London II," Christian
Century LXXXII (September 8, 1965), 1096-1097.

Sutherland, Jack. "Repellent Play from Pinter," London
Daily Worker, June 5, 1965, p. 2.

Taylor, John Russell. "A Pinter Power Struggle," Plays
and Players, XII (August 1965), 34-35.

Thirkell, Arthur. "First Night," London Daily Mirror,
June 4, 1965, p. 18.

Trewin, J.C. "Mr. Pinter Says That There's No Place Like Home," Illustrated London News, CCXLVI (June 19, 1965), 30.

"A World Out of Orbit," London Times, June 4, 1965, p. 15.

Young, B.A. "The Homecoming," London Financial Times, June 5, 1965, p. 7.

_____. "Pinter's 'Homecoming' is Staged in London," New York Times, June 4, 1965, p. 38.

January 5, 1967: Music Box Theater, New York

Bermel, Albert. "Pinter's Nightmare," New Leader, L (January 30, 1967), 30-31.

Bolton, Whitney. "Harold Pinter Play: 'The Homecoming,'" New York Morning Telegraph, January 7, 1967, p. 3.

Brustein, Robert. "Saturn Eats His Children," New Republic, CLVI (January 28, 1967), 34-36.

Cavanaugh, Arthur. "Stage," Sign, XLVI (March 1967), 31.

Chapman, John. "Pinter's 'Homecoming' a Weirdy," New York Daily News, January 6, 1967, p. 68.

Clurman, Harold. "Theatre," Nation, CCIV (January 23, 1967), 122-123.

Cohen, Marshal. "Theater 67," Partisan Review, XXXIV (Summer 1967), 436-444.

Cooke, Richard P. "Strange Family Album," Wall Street Journal, January 9, 1967, p. 12.

Croce, Arlene. "Invisible to the Naked Eye," National Review, XIX (May 2, 1967), 482-485.

Downer, Alan S. "The Doctor's Dilemma: Notes on the New York Theatre 1966-67," Quarterly Journal of Speech, LIII (October 1967), 213-223.

Gilman, Richard. "Mortal Combat," Newsweek, LXIX

(January 16, 1967), 93.

Gottfried, Martin. "'The Homecoming,'" Women's Wear
Daily, CXIV (January 6, 1967), 101.

Hewes, Henry. "Bests of the 1966-67 Theatre Season,"
Saturday Review, L (June 10, 1967), 18-22.

_____. "Pinter's Hilarious Depth Charge," Saturday
Review, L (January 21, 1967), 51.

Hipp, Edward Sothern. "'Homecoming,'" Newark Evening
News, January 6, 1967, p. 54.

Hobe. "The Homecoming," Variety, CCXLV (January 11,
1967), 72, 76.

Kemper, Robert G. "One Man's Family," Christian
Century, LXXXIV (March 1, 1967), 276-277.

Kerr, Walter. "A Pox on Shocks," New York Times,
January 15, 1967, Sec. II, p. 11.

_____. "The Theater: Pinter's 'Homecoming,'" New
York Times, January 6, 1967, p. 29.

"Land of No Holds Barred," Time, LXXXIX (January 13,
1967), 43.

"Last Words on Pinter?" New York Times, February 26,
1967, Sec. II, p. 8.

Lewis, Theophilus. "The Homecoming," America, CXVI
(March 11, 1967), 353.

Loney, Glenn. "Broadway and Off-Broadway Supplement,"
Educational Theatre Journal, XIX (May 1967), 198-204.

McCarten, John. "Amorphous Doings," New Yorker, XLII
(January 14, 1967), 48.

Morgan, Derek. "These Our Actors. . . ," Reporter, XXXVI
(February 23, 1967), 46-48.

Nadel, Norman. "'Homecoming' Unfathomable," New York
World Journal Tribune, January 6, 1967, p. 14.

Prideaux, Tom. "The Adventurous Play--Stranger to Broadway," Life, LXII (March 3, 1967), 6.

Richardson, Jack. "English Imports on Broadway," Commentary, XLIII (January 1967), 73-75.

Russell, Francis. "A Pinter Pickled Peppers," National Review, XIX (March 21, 1967), 316-317.

Sheed, Wilfrid. "The Stage," Commonweal, LXXXV (January 27, 1967), 459-460.

Simon, John. "Theatre Chronicle," Hudson Review, XX (Spring 1967), 105-114.

Watts, Richard, Jr. "Hospitality of a London Family," New York Post, January 6, 1967, p. 49.

West, Anthony. "The Homecoming, 'a Dim Crisis,'" Vogue, CXLIX (March 1, 1967), 110.

"What's Pinter Up To?" New York Times, February 5, 1967, Sec. II, p. 1.

The Basement

February 20, 1967: BBC Television, London

Banks-Smith, Nancy. "Television is not Only for Looking at," London Sun, February 21, 1967, p. 12.

Clayton, Sylvia. "'Basement' Is Ornate with No Magic," London Daily Telegraph, February 21, 1967, p. 17.

Cooper, R.W. "Mr. Pinter is a Conspiracy of Silence," London Times, February 21, 1967, p. 8.

Eastaugh, Kenneth. "A Pinter Below Par Still Has That Sure Touch of Genius," London Daily Mirror, February 21, 1967, p. 14.

Purser, Philip. "How to Take Part," London Sunday Telegraph, February 26, 1967, p. 11.

Richardson, Maurice. "Life with the Dolphins," London
    Observer, February 26, 1967, p. 25.

Wiggin, Maurice. "Bubble-gum Reputations," London
    Sunday Times, February 26, 1967, p. 50.

Landscape

April 25, 1968: BBC Third Programme, London (Radio)

Bailey, Paul. "Pinter Play," Listener, LXXIX (May 2,
    1968), 583.

Ferris, Paul. "Pop Press Intimations," London Observer,
    April 28, 1968, p. 32.

Lewis, Peter. "Turn On, Tune In to Pinter's Magic,"
    London Daily Mail, April 26, 1968, p. 16.

Rundall, Jeremy. "On the Beach," London Sunday Times,
    April 28, 1968, p. 53.

Wade, David. "New Poetry in Pinter," London Times,
    April 26, 1968, p. 9.

                July 2, 1969: Aldwych Theatre, London
                          (With Silence)

Barber, John. "Pinter Plays with Elusive Themes," London
    Daily Telegraph, July 4, 1969, p. 21.

Barnes, Clive. "Harold Pinter's Debt to James Joyce,"
    New York Times, July 25, 1969, p. 34.

Bryden, Ronald. "Pared to Privacy, Melting into Silence,"
    London Observer, July 6, 1969, p. 22.

Cushman, Robert. "Evidence and Verdict," Plays and
    Players, XVI (August 1969), 27.

Dukore, Bernard F. "The Royal Shakespeare Company,"
    Educational Theatre Journal, XXII (December 1970), 412-414.

Ghose, Zulfikar. "Ghose's London: A Valediction,"
    Hudson Review, XXII (Autumn 1969), 378, 380.

Hobson, Harold. "Paradise Lost," London Sunday Times, July 6, 1969, p. 52.

Hope-Wallace, Philip. "Pinter Plays," Manchester Guardian, July 3, 1969, p. 10.

Hughes, Catharine. "Pinter is as Pinter Does," Catholic World, CCX (December 1969), 124-126.

Jones, D. A. N. "Corruption," Listener, LXXXII (July 10, 1969), 60-61.

Kingston, Jeremy. "At the Theatre," Punch, CCLVII (July 9, 1969), 73-74.

Lambert, J. W. "Plays in Performance. London," Drama, No. 94, (Autumn 1969), 14.

Marcus, Frank. "A Couple of Half-Pinters," London Sunday Telegraph, July 6, 1969, p. 14.

_____. "Pinter: The Pauses that Refresh," New York Times, July 13, 1969, Sec. II, p. 8.

"New Plays. The Latest Pinters: Less is Less," Time, XCIV (July 18, 1969), 67.

Nightingale, Benedict. "To the Mouth of the Cave," New Statesman, LXXVIII (July 11, 1969), 57.

Norman, Barry. "Getting Nowhere in Great Style," London Daily Mail, July 4, 1969, p. 14.

Shulman, Milton. "Mini-Pinter," London Evening Standard, July 3, 1969, p. 17.

Spurling, Hilary. "Lust and Forgetfulness," Spectator, CCXXIII (July 12, 1969), 49-50.

Sutherland, Jack. "Two New Plays by Pinter," London Morning Star, July 4, 1969, p. 2.

Trewin, J. C. "Pinter's Parodies," Illustrated London News, CCL (July 12, 1969), 29.

Wardle, Irving. "Pinter Theatrical Twins in Pools of Solitude," London Times, July 4, 1969, p. 7.

Young, B.A. "Landscape--Silence," London Financial
Times, July 4, 1969, p. 3.

April 2, 1970: The Forum Theater, New York
(With Silence)

Barnes, Clive. "Stage: Pinter's Small Talk of Reality,"
New York Times, April 3, 1970, p. 43.

Clurman, Harold. "Theatre," Nation, CCX (April 20, 1970),
473-474, 476.

Gottfried, Martin. "Two New Pinter Plays," Women's Wear
Daily, CXX (April 3, 1970), 12.

Green, Harris. "Less is More, Nothing is Everything,"
New Leader, LIII (April 27, 1970), 32-33.

Hewes, Henry. "Thought Games," Saturday Review, LIII
(April 25, 1970), 16, 20.

Hipp, Edward Sothern. "Two Pinter Playlets," Newark
Evening News, April 3, 1970, p. 16.

Hobe. "Landscape & Silence," Variety, CCLVIII (April 8,
1970), 122.

Hughes, Catharine. "New York," Plays and Players, XVII
(June 1970), 16-17, 33.

Kauffmann, Stanley. "Landscape and Silence," New Republic, CLXII (April 25, 1970), 20, 31.

Kerr, Walter. "A Break With Anything Pinter Has Done
Before," New York Times, April 12, 1970, Sec. II, p. 3.

Kroll, Jack. "Harold and Sam," Newsweek, LXXV (April
13, 1970), 83.

Mishkin, Leo. "One-Act Pinter Plays Purely 'Experimental,'"
New York Morning Telegraph, April 4, 1970, p. 3.

O'Connor, John J. "The Theater. Songs and Sciences,"
Wall Street Journal, April 6, 1970, p. 18.

Oliver, Edith. "Good Shepard," New Yorker, XLVI
(April 11, 1970), 82-84.

Simon, John. "The Best of Behan," New York, III
(April 20, 1970), 62.

Watt, Douglas. "Some of Pinter's Magic Turned On at the
Forum," New York Daily News, April 3, 1970, p. 64.

Watts, Richard. "Pinter Without the Menace," New York
Post, April 3, 1970, p. 38.

Miscellaneous Reviews

"Destruction of a Tramp," London Times, February 11,
1964, p. 13. [The Caretaker done by the Cambridge
(England) Amateur Dramatic Club.]

"Experimental Theatre Co. production of The Birthday
Party," London Times, November 28, 1963, p. 17. [The
Birthday Party done November 25, 1963, at Oxford,
England.]

Hewes, Henry. "The Company It's Kept," Saturday Review,
LII (November 15, 1969), 20. [The Homecoming done in
Minneapolis by the Minnesota Theatre Company.]

_____. "The 'Frisco Kids," Saturday Review, XLIV
(August 26, 1961), 26. [The Birthday Party done in San
Francisco.]

"Two Pairs of Lovers," London Times, February 28, 1964,
p. 16. [The Collection done at King's College, London.]

146